AF450316

No other gods

Why undivided loyalty to the One and only living God matters in these days

THE TEN COMMANDMENTS SERIES

Marja Verschoor-Meijers

Even if there are so-called "gods," whether in heaven or on earth, and even though there are many of these "gods" and "lords," yet there is for us only one God, the Father, who is the Creator of all things and for whom we live; and there is only one Lord, Jesus Christ, through whom all things were created and through whom we live.

1 Corinthians 8:5-6

Table of contents

1st Commandment

And God spoke all these words, saying: "I am the Lord your God, who brought you out of the land of Egypt, out of the house of bondage. You shall have no other gods before Me."

Exodus 20:1-3 (NKJV)

Introduction

Happy are those who trust the Lord, who do not turn to idols or join those who worship false gods.

Psalm 40:4

My husband and I both grew up in Christian homes. Our parents kept the religious traditions passed on from their parents and grandparents and passed them on to us. At the age of sixteen we were more interested in the things the world had to offer and we stopped going to church.

We never denied the existence of God, but somehow we had never made a conscious decision to be a follower of Christ either. Personal faith was not being preached in our denomination and, at that time in our lives, we thought our upbringing was kind of enough to call ourselves Christians. When we started traveling all over the world with our backpacks, we would even defend our Christian heritage. Surely, we were not Hindus, Buddhists, or Muslims for that matter.

We had one foot in the Kingdom of God and one foot in the world, so to speak. We knew the basic biblical values, but we did not pursue a life of godliness. As most people in Western societies, believers or not, we were familiar with the Ten Commandments. In many countries they are the basis for the judicial system. In a way they form the 'moral code' for a safe and healthy society.

Now, this 'moral code' is being attacked from all possible sides. As a matter of fact, everything based on God's Word and His principles is being attacked and contradicted. The ferocious lobby for the removal of God's standard for a safe and healthy society is rooted in the evil drive to distance people from the heart of God and from His Word. An entire generation lost touch with the core values of Christianity and that in itself provides a perfect base for the enemy to enter family life, church life, cultural life, and political arenas. We have given the enemy, often by Supreme Court ruling, a free hand to do his thing… alienate people from the very God that created them.

This alienation from God Himself and from the values and principles as described in His Word is not as liberating as expected. It gives way to the downfall of civilization. It gives way to the destruction of healthy societies and traditional family life. It gives way to the birth of a new generation that is confused about almost everything: truth, purpose, identity, climate etc. The apostle James describes the current state of affairs like this:

If you need wisdom, ask our generous God, and he will give it to you. He will not rebuke you for asking. But when you ask him, be sure that your faith is in God alone. Do not waver, for a person with divided loyalty is as unsettled as a wave of the sea that is blown and tossed by the wind. Such people should not expect to receive anything from the Lord. Their loyalty is divided between God and the world, and they are unstable in everything they do (James 1:5-8, NLT).

When our loyalty is divided between God and the world we will end up being unstable in everything we do. Think about that! An unstable life, or an unstable society for that matter, is the result of divided loyalty. Simply put, we cannot have one foot in the Kingdom of God and one foot in the world. We cannot serve two masters. We cannot serve both God and the world. Bob Dylan sang it: 'You gotta serve somebody.' This is an elementary truth. People may think they serve no one and call themselves atheists or agnostics, but the fact of the matter is, we all serve someone. We either serve God or other gods, as we will see in this book.

'No other gods' is the tenth and final book in this series and it deals with the first commandment in which God warns us not to have other gods before Him. The first commandment is so much more than just a rule, a law, a decree, or even a mere prohibition. In essence it is a call to holiness. My free interpretation comes down to 'No compromise', which is quite radical in a world full of compromises, full of choices, and full of alternatives. We want it all and we can have it all, but in the process we are becoming more and more confused and less and less focused. Major confusion, whether mentally, emotionally, physically, or spiritually, is the disease of our time.

As Christians we should never mix our faith in God with the enticements of this world. This is dangerous ground… unstable ground and the Bible warns us repeatedly not to go that way. 'You shall have no other gods before me' means so much more than just refraining from worshiping idols. Of course, we have no other gods besides the Lord in our lives, if all is well. But let's be honest here; how big is the influence of the world in our lives? Are we refusing to let the world corrupt us? At times it seems this evil world is closing in on us and that can be a frightening feeling. But there is hope, there is always hope!

This book is a call for undivided loyalty towards the Lord. It is a call to honor the God of Abraham, Isaac, and Jacob as the supreme God, the Creator of heaven and earth, and to honor His Word. It is also a call to not be ignorant about the destructive influence of principalities and powers, demons and deities, false religious practices and forces of darkness. We must come out of the spiritual battle we find ourselves in with victory and a strong faith.

We must decide now to stand up and take back what the enemy has stolen from us. Let's make it our aim to live as God intended it from the beginning: for us to be blessed and fruitful, content and encouraged, thankful and inspirational for generations to come.

Please, pray the following prayer out loud before you read any further. It will definitely help you to receive all that the Holy Spirit wants to whisper in your ears.

Dear Father in Heaven,

Thank You that You are supreme over all other gods. Thank You that there is no greater power in the universe than Your love, Your grace, and Your forgiveness, which overrules the darkness. Thank You for giving me hope and an eternal perspective.

Holy Spirit, help me to live out my life in devotion to God alone. Help me to be an example to the people around me, may they see Jesus in me. Open my eyes for the wonderful truths in Your Word, I want to learn more and become wise amidst the madness I see in this world. I honor You as Teacher and Counselor, knowing that Jesus did send You to be with us until the end of time. I ask all of this in the mighty name of Jesus. Amen.

Marja Verschoor-Meijers

1

He is supreme

Do not abandon me and worship idols; do not make gods of metal and worship them. I am the Lord your God.

Leviticus 19:4

Most restaurants in India are basic. Well, at least the ones where backpackers like to go. A few bare tables and wobbly chairs, hardly any decorations except for some pictures of Hindu gods and goddesses. And there is music… loud music.

I know this, not because I watched National Geographic, but because I have been there. Back in the nineties of the previous century we were backpackers, quite radical ones I should add. My boyfriend (who later became my husband) and I traveled all over the globe for months at the time. We would go back home to work temporary jobs so that we would not run out of money and at the same time save up for our next trip.

We lived like this for quite some years and visited more than fifty countries on several continents. Traveling with a backpack was an adventure, certainly back then when there was no internet or cell phone connection. We were on our own with a travel guide in our hands. Paperback of course.

I remember how we were in one of such restaurants, enjoying delicious curry and fresh baked naan bread. Among the pictures of the gods lining the walls was a picture of Jesus. Well, the Jesus as most people in the Western world imagine Him to be like. Sort of a long-haired friendly hippy with a beard and kindness shining out of His eyes. Although we were not believers then, it seemed easy to love Him at first sight. I remember asking the restaurant owner why Jesus was there, among all the other gods. What did He have to do with Hinduism? The answer was simple. 'He was a good and wise man, we like Him.'

It turned out that some people in India, like the restaurant owner, just kept adding mystical figures, modern-day guru's, and divine entities to their list of gods. Mind you, Hinduism acknowledges various deities and millions of gods and goddesses. One more or less never hurts. We must have looked at the restaurant owner quite questionably, because he added: 'You can never have enough gods.'

That logic was beyond our understanding, to be honest. We were raised in a Christian home and had always understood that one God was sufficient for everything!

One God, the Creator of the universe, the King of kings and Lord of lords had no serious competition, as far as we knew. I mean, if you need a million or more gods to make life livable, isn't there something wrong with the power and presence of these so-called gods?

Just think about it, to be in need of a different god when the weather needs to change, when there is a food or water shortage, when sickness or poverty knocks on your door, when in need of protection, guidance, or direction. My goodness, that would make life quite complicated. For people who are used to the concept of polytheism, the belief in or worship of more than one god, this is quite normal and acceptable. The opposite is just as true for the ones growing up in monotheistic religions, such as Christianity, Judaism, and Islam. Who needs other gods if your God is supreme over all others?

Well, that would have been a good question for the ancient Israelites, who were chosen, cherished, and loved by God, and yet were frequently running after other gods. We can read about their disastrous spiritual escapades throughout the Old Testament. We can read stories of individuals who worshiped other gods but also how Israel, as a nation, corporately sinned against the commandment not to have other gods. As a matter of fact, idolatry (the worshiping of idols) was a consistent pattern throughout the history of Israel. Only after the exile did the idolatrous worship of other gods cease among the Jews for some time.

In the Torah, the first five books of the Bible, it is made clear on many occasions that there was no God like Yahweh, the God of Israel, and that it would greatly benefit the people if they worshiped and obeyed Him only. In Deuteronomy 10:17 for example, it is stated:

The Lord your God is supreme over all gods and over all powers. He is great and mighty, and he is to be obeyed. He does not show partiality, and he does not accept bribes.

Supreme over all gods. I find that a very intriguing idea. So, there *are* other gods then! As I wrote earlier in this chapter, I grew up with the idea that there was only one God, the God of Israel, the God of the Bible. In our home and our church, we never talked about other gods, demons, evil spirits, or the devil for that matter. Such topics were nonexistent in the denomination we grew up in. Looking back, I can see the danger of such ignorance. As a matter of fact, I believe the devil laughs at such ignorance, it is part of his plan to paralyze the church.

God is supreme over other gods, as we just read… so, who are these other gods? Does the Bible talk about other gods? Yes, it does, quite often actually. Let me put it this way, if there were no other gods, there would be no need for the first commandment which would make the other nine worthless, or questionable to say the least. Let's take the first commandment, as written by the finger of God, very seriously. Maybe it will help to put a fresh look at the words. What exactly does the first commandment say? Just go with me to Exodus 20:1-3 (NKJV), where we can read the following:

And God spoke all these words, saying: "I am the Lord your God, who brought you out of the land of Egypt, out of the house of bondage. You shall have no other gods before Me."

You shall have no other gods before Me. Amen. That is quite clear and would make for a very short sermon about undivided allegiance to God. But more than that, the commandment wouldn't be needed if no other gods existed. Well, that is my quite humble but firm conclusion. So, that takes us to the topic of this last book in the series about the Ten Commandments in the 21st century: the warning against other gods and the call to live an uncompromised life of faith and loyalty towards the God of Abraham, Isaac, and Jacob.

The first commandment should challenge our thinking on several points. God identifies Himself as the Great I Am, as the God who brought the Israelites out of the house of bondage. He is still the same God today. He has not changed. He brings people out of bondage each and every day all over the world. He is the One who still delivers people from slavery. Slavery to sin, to drugs and alcohol, to pornography, gambling and greed, to poverty, anger, selfishness, and fear, just to name a few.

I don't know what your house of bondage was or is, just remember that He will always be the Lord our God who wants all people to walk in freedom. And that precious and costly freedom is exactly why the scripture continues with 'you shall have no other gods before me'. God basically said: 'It's Me or nothing!' A very clear and simple warning against divided loyalty when it comes to faith in God.

The first commandment talks about the existence of other gods which is kind of weird in the context of monotheistic religions, as I mentioned before. It tells me that we have to look at the first commandment in a much broader perspective. Yes, there are other gods, and no, we should not have them before God.

The Wycliffe Bible says it like this: 'Thou shalt not have alien gods before me (You shall not have foreign [other] gods in place of me/instead of me).' I like that word 'alien' which means belonging to a foreign country but also 'unfamiliar and disturbing' or 'distasteful'. That makes sense, God wants to be a personal God to both Jew and gentile. He wants to be known by name, by His Word, by His Son Jesus, and by the Holy Spirit who will be with us forever.

Serving or worshiping alien gods therefore is equivalent to refusing His outstretched hand and His eternal love. Devotion to other gods will eventually take the place of the God we should love with all of our heart and all of our mind and all of our strength.

Maybe you are thinking this book is not of interest to you. Simply because you serve no other gods, you are loyal to the God of the Bible. And besides, it is an Old Testament commandment and we live in a different time now. Well, please hear me out. I promise you will get something out of this book. It could be

- some insights that might bring refreshment in your own faith walk;
- a fresh understanding that may help you to teach others and to point others into the right direction;
- new knowledge about the so-called gods that are currently operating in our society, culture, religion, politics, and our governments.

There is a reason why the last book in this series is about the first commandment. A commandment that is of major importance to all of us today. A commandment that will help us to keep standing in faith while the world as we know it continues to crumble. All the lessons we learned from the previous books will culminate in this one. I pray that the words I wrote will bless you.

Meditate on the following:

- *What is my personal view of the God of the Bible?*
- *How would I describe Him to an unbeliever?*

Journal your thoughts:

2

He is holy

Lord, who among the gods is like you? Who is like you, wonderful in holiness? Who can work miracles and mighty acts like yours?

Exodus 15:11

We came upon the pilgrimage site by accident. We were traveling down south in Europe in our old Citroën camper van and came to the beautiful province of Andalusia in Spain. I don't know if you have ever been there, but life in Andalusia, as is the case with most of the regions in Spain, is rich with folklore tradition, cultural heritage, and religious practices. Quite a sight to see!

We came to the small town of El Rocío where the dwelling place and the statue of 'Our Lady of El Rocío' attract one million pilgrims from all over Spain, each year. The festival and the pilgrimage last for several days. For people who do not have a Catholic background, it is quite strange to see young and old alike dancing in procession while carrying and sometimes even kissing a statue. We watched with interest and took it all in. The adoration seemed a bit over the top to us at the time but later on the thought occurred to me that kissing a statue is simply a way to acknowledge and express love and respect for the person or idea behind the statue. I mean, I have seen people kissing the Oscar and Golden Globe, I have seen people kissing the World Soccer Gold Cup, I have seen people kissing the Bible, the ground at Tel Aviv airport in Israel, and the feet of a statue of Jesus. People who do this are happy, excited, overcome by emotions and often thankful, blowing their kisses for the world to see. We don't think much of it.

People have always been looking for ways to express their love and devotion for their family, their tribe, their sports, their country, their gods, and so on, and so on. Even so, humans have always sought out ways to express their love for God and the Bible. They have done so in composing music, painting pictures, building cathedrals, and yeah, maybe even in kissing statues of the Virgin Mary. In that sense, I realize we are all different and we all grew up with different traditions and rituals.

The problem occurs when our devotion to created things overtakes our devotion to the One who is supreme over it all. Now, there is nothing new under the sun indeed, for the apostle Paul penned a severe warning against such practices. In Romans 1:22-23 (NIV) we can read the following:

Although they claimed to be wise, they became fools and exchanged the glory of the immortal God for images made to look like a mortal human being and birds and animals and reptiles.

How do people become fools? How does a society become foolish for that matter? By exchanging the glory of God for images, for idols, for statues. This is exactly what the people of Israel did over and over again, as we can read throughout the Bible. Although their journey as a chosen people was (and still is) very specific, in some ways it is not so different from ours. We are all sojourners and somehow we all share the same mistakes. Therefore, the warning about 'other gods' is not just an Old Testament topic, it is a timeless universal one. The words of the apostle Paul remind me of Psalm 14:1 (NLT):

Only fools say in their hearts, "There is no God."

Who wants to be called a fool? Not me.

In this context it would be very interesting to read 1 Corinthians chapter 10 about Israel's idolatry, which is a clear lesson for us today. More about that further on in this book. The apostle Paul starts that chapter by saying, 'I do not want you to be ignorant'. We don't want to be ignorant, do we? The experiences of the ancient Israelites serve as examples to us. Everything has been recorded to teach us, to edify us, and to encourage us to live a life that is pleasing to God.

The mistakes we make and the sins we commit cannot keep the love of God at a distance. As a matter of fact, they are the reason He extends His grace and forgiveness. We can see that concept throughout biblical history. Although the ancient Israelites made a lot of mistakes, they were and are the object of God's love:

Look, the highest heavens and the earth and everything in it all belong to the Lord your God. Yet the Lord chose your ancestors as the objects of his love. And he chose you, their descendants, above all other nations, as is evident today (Deuteronomy 10:14-15, NLT).

Make no mistake about it, God has not changed His mind when it comes to the people of Israel. His love covers a multitude of sins, even idolatry, and it still does. Let me put it this way, the whole world is the object of His love! We can read that in probably the most famous verse in the entire Bible, John 3:16,

For God loved the world so much that he gave his only Son, so that everyone who believes in him may not die but have eternal life.

Whether ancient Israelite, modern-day Jew or gentile, we all have been given the free will to respond to His love or to ignore it. We all have been given the free will to put

Him first in our lives and worship Him only, or to give Him a lesser place among all the other things and people that demand so much of our time, money, and devotion. It wouldn't hurt to ask ourselves from time to time whether we love Him now as we did at first or whether our first love has been quenched by what the world has to offer? Remaining faithful is a core value for believers. Our gratefulness and devotion towards God expresses itself in our faithfulness towards God. I wrote about that in my book 'First Love'.

The first commandment is clear: we should have no other gods before Him. The real question for believers today is: Is He indeed first in everything we think, say or do? When in pain, do we go to Him first? When in trouble, do we first take it to prayer and ask for advice? When worried, do we go to Him to look for peace? When about to make a big decision, do we seek His counsel, do we search His Word?

It is so easy to say that we have no other gods and maybe we even point our religious finger at different cultures and religions calling them idolatrous. Throughout this book I would like to call for an introspective look into our own lives and habits and see whether we truly put Him first in everything. I am sure you have heard Christians say after they had done all they could do in their own strength: 'All we can do is pray now'. Why not start with prayer? Why not seek God first? And if He remains silent, we can still go to a doctor, a banker, a specialist, a therapist, or a counselor.

I sincerely believe we are in serious need of reversing our actions when it comes to putting God first. I am not talking about what we do in church, I am talking about our daily lives. No other gods. It doesn't leave much room to live life trusting all the conveniences and back-ups we have surrounded ourselves with.

God alone deserves the glory and honor for He alone is holy. Let me put it this way, He deserves our kisses and praise!

Meditate on the following:

- *How would I describe God's love for the world?*
- *My thoughts about 'other gods'…*

Journal your thoughts:

3

He is glorious

Has any nation ever traded its gods for new ones, even though they are not gods at all? Yet my people have exchanged their glorious God for worthless idols!

Jeremiah 2:11 (NLT)

We were backpacking throughout South-East Asia and after several weeks exploring the island of Java in Indonesia we took the ferry to the next island, beautiful and exotic Bali. We rented a small 100cc motorcycle to travel around the island that is known for its beautiful nature, terraced rice paddies, colorful culture, and superb cuisine.

Bali is also known as 'Land of the gods'. The main religion on the island is Hinduism, although Islam has been spreading quickly in past decades. The Hindu religion as practiced on the island is quite different from the Hinduism one can find in Thailand and India for example. It is more a form of what we would call Animism. Everything has a deity that lives inside or is possessed by a deity. The festive calendar in Bali is therefore full of religious events of all sorts to honor different gods and those events call for a wide variety of rituals.

I remember that almost every house and dwelling had a tiny temple in front, just like you see mailboxes in the USA or bird feeders. These little temples serve as locations for the daily food offerings to the gods, spirits, and ancestors. Home owners will place a small woven bamboo container in the temple filled with rice, flowers, incense, sweets, fruits, spices, and sometimes even a cigarette, which makes you wonder.

These offerings are a gesture of gratitude towards the gods of the island. I don't remember exactly what is being done with the food offered to the gods, whether the homeowner throws it away the next day or whether it gets eaten by birds. Somehow, a new offering gets placed in the mini temple each day. The pleasing of the gods is part of daily life on the island of Bali and the worship of gods and deities is interwoven in society.

Surely, not all inhabitants participate and hold on to the ancient beliefs, but even as a tourist you can see and feel that the atmosphere is highly influenced by all kinds of religious practices. Although times have changed somewhat since we were there, in general Buddhists, Christians, Hindus, Muslims, and Animists live together without major problems on this small island and in that sense the island propagates coexistence. Coexistence means living together peacefully despite differences, which may be in the realm of goals, values, ideology, religion, race, nationality, ethnicity, culture, and other domains. Nowadays it is also a popular religious belief in Israel.

The existence of other gods and religions is not new, of course. The first time other gods are mentioned in the Bible is in Genesis 31, so way before the Law was given to Moses. In Genesis we can read the account of Jacob fleeing from his uncle Laban. His wife Rachel stole the household gods of her father and put them in a camel's saddlebag and was sitting on them. Laban searched through the whole tent, but did not find the household idols. Now Jacob knew nothing about this and when he found out his wife had indeed the household gods in her possession, he told his family and all who were with him to get rid of the foreign gods and to purify themselves and put on clean clothes. It was that serious of an offense.

Foreign gods were a danger and they needed to be disposed of. We can read in Genesis 35:4 how that happened:

So they gave Jacob all the foreign gods that they had and also the earrings that they were wearing. He buried them beneath the oak tree near Shechem.

The other gods, that were a constant distraction and danger to the loyalty of the Israelites, were the gods of other nations and religions that surrounded them. They were gods made by human hands, also called idols or statues. We can read that in Psalm 135:15,

The gods of the nations are made of silver and gold; they are formed by human hands.

Many people worshiped created gods instead of the Creator Himself. I believe it is still like this today. People worship nature instead of the One who called it all into being. People worship knowledge and academic accomplishments instead of the One from whom all wisdom flows. So it was in ancient times when the peoples surrounding the Israelites worshiped man-made gods. So-called gods that couldn't talk, see, or hear, yet the people worshiped them with all of their strength and might, expecting a sign of life from these motionless statues, idols, or pillars.

God warned the Israelites repeatedly not to adapt such practices. He gave them clear warnings as well as instructions on how to deal with foreign gods. In Exodus 23:24-26 for example:

Do not bow down to their gods or worship them, and do not adopt their religious practices. Destroy their gods and break down their sacred stone pillars. If you worship me, the Lord your God, I will bless you with food and water and take away all your sicknesses. In your land no

woman will have a miscarriage or be without children. I will give you long lives.

He made it quite clear, 'Worship Me and I will bless you!' Why would they, or us for that matter, ignore such a command? It is much better to have the blessing of the Lord on our lives than the curses of other gods. It seems like an easy choice to make, yet the Israelites wavered in their decision to follow no other god but the Great I Am. Read with me as we continue in chapter 24:32-33,

Do not make any agreement with them or with their gods. Do not let those people live in your country; if you do, they will make you sin against me. If you worship their gods, it will be a fatal trap for you.

It will be a fatal trap for you. Worshiping other gods than the Creator of heaven and earth is a trap, a fatal one. It was a trap back then, it is still a trap today. When anyone or anything becomes the object of our worship and devotion, we are walking into a trap. The object of our worship may not be a statue or sacred pillar as mentioned in the Bible, but it could be an ideology, a philosophy, a financial plan, an idea, a leader of a group, religion or political party, or even the pharmaceutical industry. When we expect blessings from any other source than God Himself, we are being deceived and ultimately trapped.

If we expect human effort or provision to save us, to deliver us, to heal us, or to give us a better life… we are in for a surprise. We will end up being disappointed, disillusioned, and distracted. God has promised in His Word to give us all such things if we seek Him and His Kingdom first.

Seek the Kingdom of God above all else, and live righteously, and he will give you everything you need (Matthew 6:33, NLT).

He will give us everything we need, how wonderful. And yes, of course He will use people in His service which is absolutely awesome. So I am not speaking against the leader, the banker, or the pharmacist personally. I am speaking against putting our hope and trust in people, remedies, economics, and politics.

Meditate on the following:

- *Whom or what do I admire greatly?*
- *How does that admiration relate to my relationship with God?*

Journal your thoughts:

4

He is gracious

All nations will remember the Lord. From every part of the world they will turn to him; all races will worship him. The Lord is king, and he rules the nations.

Psalm 22:27-28

The country of Malaysia is blessed with jungles, forests, beaches, and mountains. It is truly a beautiful place on earth with a rich culture and heritage and we thoroughly enjoyed traveling around this colorful nation with our backpacks. The people are friendly, transportation is easily available, hostels can be found everywhere, and the food served is certainly delicious.

We visited the tea plantations of central Malaysia, the capital Kuala Lumpur, as well as some of the tiny islands that are scattered along the east coast. It was there that we had an encounter with Komodo dragons also called monitor lizards, the largest lizard known to be living on earth. Quite a site to see and I can imagine why some people would rather visit a city. Nature holds a vast array of surprises in that region of the world, believe me. We lost track of the various kinds of insects, critters, and snakes we encountered during our travels. Not my friends really. City visits have their charm too.

One day we stood in front of an impressive mosque in Kuala Lumpur. Upon entering we had to leave our shoes amidst the thousands of pairs of slippers and sandals that were lining up the walls in the entrance way. Before going further I needed to cover my head and once inside it turned out there were separate men's and women's sections. Wow, all those rules, it felt a bit suffocating despite the beauty of the interior. I was afraid to make a mistake. On the other hand… I understood each religion has its own rules and rituals and visitors are always asked and expected to show proper respect. So, inside this magnificent building people were kneeling down and in a way that was intriguing. Bowing down in reverence and awe before their god.

The thought hit me that as Christians we do not bow down so easily, we rather stand up for Jesus to make our requests known. Bowing down, face to the ground, is a universal sign of respect and the Bible holds many examples of such forms of reverence and awe. In my book 'True Worshipers', I proposed bowing down again for God during our times of private and corporate worship. It is a sign of a humble attitude and it certainly elevates God and thus makes us less important. Therefore worship is a core value for all believers.

Anyway, back to Kuala Lumpur. The prayers uttered in that mosque, and in any mosque for that matter, are not random, they are specific and need to be prayed at certain times, facing the city of Mecca. The rules are quite strict. 'Well Marja, Christianity has a lot of rules as well, what's wrong with that?' you may ask. A good question, certainly in a book about one of the Ten Commandments. If you have read some of my previous books, you must have noticed that in this series we do not focus on what we cannot or should not do, but on what the Holy Spirit wants to do through us. We do not focus on the rules, but on the spiritual principles hidden within the letter of the Law, principles that will lead to fulfillment of the Law.

Before continuing with several more memories about our travels around the world and sharing my thoughts about the 1st commandment, I would like to share a bit more about the point of view I have taken in writing about God's commandments. Many believers, and maybe you are one of them, regard law and grace as opposites and discussions can get rather fanatic on both sides. Believe me, I have been in the middle of many intense debates. Personally, I strongly believe it is not law *or* grace, but law *and* grace as both come together and find their fulfillment in Jesus Christ.

Think about it, God's plan and desire for mankind, for every single person on the face of the earth, is salvation. Salvation is a beautiful word with a deep meaning, namely: rescue or deliverance from sin and the consequences thereof (death and destruction). Behind God's graceful rescue mission is the offer of eternal life. An offer we can simply accept by faith in His Son, Jesus Christ—yes, through faith, not through obeying rules.

If you have read any other books in this series, you will remember that merely obeying the commandments won't get us very far. People tried that for thousands of years, yet they kept on sinning and distanced themselves from a holy God. We can read about that struggle in Romans 9:31-32 (NLT),

The people of Israel, who tried so hard to get right with God by keeping the Law, never succeeded. Why not? Because they were trying to get right with God by keeping the Law instead of by trusting in him…

Keeping the Law cannot put anyone right with God. The Old Testament law cannot bridge the gap between God and people. Only Jesus Christ can do that. The Law therefore was not given to bring about salvation, but to amplify the need for it.

Salvation brings us in harmony with God. The heart of salvation is the restoration of friendship between God and mankind (which the Bible calls reconciliation) and it is only possible through faith in His Son, Jesus Christ. I want to make it absolutely clear that faith in Jesus Christ is the only way to befriend God the Father. I realize people try to get in contact with the Divine through meditation, spiritual exercise or wearing magic stones around their neck, but truly… works (our efforts) will not get us there and this is true for any kind of religious practice, no matter what cult or religion people follow. God wants our love, not our works. So, I do not and will not preach salvation through works.

However, I do preach a genuine love for God's Word and His laws. Yes, for His laws too. One of the reasons for doing so lies in my conviction that speaking negatively about God's law or ignoring His commandments will block any dialogue with Jewish people who often regard the Torah (the first five books in the Bible, the books written by Moses) as highly valuable and trustworthy. What many Jewish people have against Christianity is the fact, among other things, that we do not respect the old writings, that we often act like the Torah (which means 'teaching') has been replaced by the New Testament writings. Disrespect ruins relationships. We simply cannot afford to distance our religious views from the people that received the Good News in the first place! I have therefore done my best to share spiritual revelation with respect to the written laws.

So, salvation is the result of God's grace *and* our faith. Let me use an analogy to illustrate this. Let's say there is this beautiful girl who is dating an honest and bright young man. He loves her genuinely and one day he decides to ask her to marry him. He comes up to the girl with a simple yet delicate ring. Kneeling down he offers himself to her… will you take me? Now, the girl is a little skeptical. She finds it hard to believe he really loves her. She finds it difficult to accept that he is truly laying down his life to be with her. Is she worthy of his love? She hesitates, but later realizes that only when she accepts the ring, trusting that he will be a good and faithful husband, their new life together can start.

So it is with God who, in His grace, offers us a new life (salvation from the old messed up life) but in order to enter that life we must say yes. We must accept that invitation in faith… believing and trusting that He will do what He has promised. God's grace is a free gift, but it has to be accepted in faith. Ephesians 2:8-9 explains this quite simply,

For it is by God's grace that you have been saved through faith. It is not the result of your own efforts, but God's gift, so that no one can boast about it.

It is never in the things we do, it comes by surrendering in faith. Trying to obey the teachings without accepting the forgiveness of our sins would only lead to frustration. Imitating Jesus without accepting His grace would lead us nowhere. That is why the books in this series are not so much about keeping or obeying the Law but all about fulfilling the Law the way Jesus did. I have reasons to believe that some people in Jesus' time were hoping the Law would be annulled, just as much as many people in our time want to live without any rules or regulations. It is not clear what their expectations or questions were, but Jesus tells them:

Do not think that I have come to do away with the Law of Moses and the teachings of the prophets. I have not come to do away with them, but to make their teachings come true (Matthew 5:17).

The NLT says 'don't misunderstand why I have come.' If Jesus said He did not come to do away with the Law, why would we do otherwise? If Jesus said He came to make their teachings come true, why wouldn't we follow His example? Jesus did not do away with the Law; He fulfilled the Law, He made the teachings come true. Some translations say He completed the Torah. I love that expression. In modern (technical) terms we would say that He upgraded the Torah. I can really appreciate the way the apostle Paul explains it in Romans 10:4 (NLT),

For Christ has already accomplished the purpose for which the Law was given. As a result, all who believe in him are made right with God.

He accomplished the purpose for which the Law was given: obtaining righteousness or, in everyday language, being on right terms with God. Because of what Jesus did, everyone can get right with God through believing, not through keeping or obeying the Law. When Jesus said He had come to accomplish the purpose of the Law, He did not delete or do away with the Law. On the contrary, He emphasized the fact that not a single letter or comma would disappear, not until the end of all things. That is not a word or warning that should scare us. On the contrary, it should make us curious to find out how to apply the Law in our day and age.

The first commandment as we can find it in Exodus 20:1-3 (NKJV) goes like this,

And God spoke all these words, saying: "I am the Lord your God, who brought you out of the land of Egypt, out of the house of bondage. You shall have no other gods before Me."

Now, maybe you say: 'Well, I have never worshiped other gods, I have no idols in my life, I believe in the God of the Bible, I have accepted Jesus… Why should I read this book?' Let me ask you a question. Do you love God above all else? I sincerely believe that the New Testament fulfillment of the commandments can be found in Matthew 22:36-40 where one of the Pharisees tried to trap Jesus with a question and basically asked: 'Which is the greatest commandment in the Law?' The answer Jesus gives is quite interesting:

Jesus answered, "'Love the Lord your God with all your heart, with all your soul, and with all your mind.' This is the greatest and the most important commandment. The second most important commandment is like it: 'Love your neighbor as you love yourself.' The whole Law of Moses and the teachings of the prophets depend on these two commandments."

He quoted the Law as mentioned in Deuteronomy 6:5. Saying we do not have any other gods before Him is one thing. It is another thing to be able to say that we love Him with all that is within us. To love God with all our heart, with all our soul, and with all our mind means to obey Him in our decisions, in our thinking, in our emotions.

Not being corrupted by the world is what it truly means to fulfill the ancient commandment. Not being corrupted by the world, in other words being undividedly loyal. The Bible calls such an attitude and lifestyle 'pure and genuine religion'.

What God the Father considers to be pure and genuine religion is this: to take care of orphans and widows in their suffering and to keep oneself from being corrupted by the world (James 1:27).

Meditate on the following:

- *Law and grace, how do they match?*
- *How would I describe pure and genuine religion in my own words.*

Journal your thoughts:

5

He is worthy

... and the prophets spoke in the name of Baal, wasting their time on worthless idols.

Jeremiah 2:8b (NLT)

We screamed and yelled and raised our hands at the concert, while jumping up and down the waves of loud music. Sweat streaming down our faces, voices raw from smoke, and eyes tired from the flickering spotlights.

In our younger years we had a taste for a certain kind of music, such as blues, rock and a little metal. We would spend our money, as many young adults would do, on concert tickets, albums, t-shirts, and other paraphernalia. When we came to faith, it was amazing to me how fast we lost interest in these things. No one told us to, no one pushed us. It was the Holy Spirit who cultivated a new desire within us, a desire for music (as well as movies and books) that would honor the Lord. The hunt for music that would elevate God was on.

Of course, music plays an important role in people's lives, especially when we are young and feel we can identify with certain music styles, lyrics, or even the crowd that it attracts. There is nothing wrong with that. God loves music and He invented it. However, the devotion to certain types of music or a specific band or artist can take on the form of idolatry. Of course, we often don't realize we are on the path of idolatry when we are showing our devotion to certain musicians, bands, or even music itself. We may be ignorant, but the devil isn't. He puts his works in plain sight, for all to see… that is, if our eyes are open. Let's be honest here, we even have TV shows called 'Idols'. Quite a clear message, isn't it?

There is so much more behind the seemingly innocent worship of music. For example, 'Gods of Metal' is a big Italian metal festival, held annually since 1997. It takes place in early summer and attracts quite a crowd. Gods of Metal, quite an interesting name for a festival. Especially when we go back thousands of years to the time when the Israelites were on their way to the promised land. God specifically told them:

Do not make gods of metal and worship them (Exodus 34:17).

Now, of course with 'metal' God referred to an ore the earth provided and not to music (well, that is my guess), but this prohibition is probably what inspired the organizers of this modern-day metal festival. In ancient times people made gods out of gold, silver, bronze and other metals. The story of the gold bull-calf is undoubtedly one of the most familiar stories in the Old Testament when it comes to worshiping a metal god. The story can be found in Exodus 32. Verses 1-4 led up to the disastrous events in the desert.

When the people saw that Moses had not come down from the mountain but was staying there a long time, they gathered around Aaron and said to him, "We do not know what has happened to this man Moses, who led us out of Egypt; so make us a god to lead us." Aaron said to them, "Take off the gold earrings which your wives, your sons, and your daughters are wearing, and bring them to me." So all the people took off their gold earrings and brought them to Aaron. He took the earrings, melted them, poured the gold into a mold, and made a gold bull-calf. The people said, "Israel, this is our god, who led us out of Egypt!"

Just imagine, the same people who had experienced the parting of the Red Sea and the deliverance from slavery in Egypt, were looking at a statue made of gold and proclaimed the statue to be their god. That may seem like a far out idea to us who live in a totally different time and I am sure it was a far out idea to their leader Moses who just had an encounter with the true and living God!

Biblical history tells us that throughout the centuries people from all cultures and backgrounds have proclaimed lifeless objects to be gods and goddesses. And the other way around of course: making lifeless objects to represent the gods they believed in. People were in need of gods they could see and touch and so they preferred lifeless idols above the one true living God who is Spirit, and therefore could not be seen.

The desire to experience God, to actually be in His presence, to see and hear Him, is a desire God Himself put in people. He created people with a longing to seek Him. Throughout the ages mankind has come up with ways to feel 'connected'. Let's not forget that God wants to be near us even more so. Seeking and desiring to be in the presence of God is a core value for believers and His presence is to be found in His name, in His Word, and in fellowship with His Holy Spirit. I wrote extensively about that in my book 'In My Name'.

Anyway, Israel was surrounded by pagan nations who believed worshiping several gods was better than worshiping just a single god and that idea was somehow attractive to the Israelites. Over and over again they received warnings not to walk into that trap. The prophet Samuel, for example, made it quite clear:

Don't go after false gods; they cannot help you or save you, for they are not real (1 Samuel 12:21).

False gods are gods, but they are not real. Maybe that sounds strange, let me therefore use an example from everyday life. Certain Asian companies manufacture cheap copies of expensive watches, purses, jackets, and shoes. I am sure you have all seen such products. Yes, you might hold a nice looking watch in your hand, it is a watch for sure, it might even work. But... it is not the real thing. It is not a real Rolex. Yes, you might look at a nice pair of sneakers, they may be your size, they may even feel comfortable. But... they are not the real thing, they are not real Nikes. The same is true for the false gods, they are there, they may even have names and attributes ascribed to them. But... they are not real. As Samuel said, 'they cannot help you or save you.'

It must have been a real shocker for Moses to find out that the Israelites worshiped a golden calf and declared that lifeless statue to be the god that led them out of the house of bondage. While leading the Israelites through the desert, it is quite interesting to note that although Moses acknowledged God as being the supreme God of Israel, he questioned Him about these so-called other gods. Were they real? Could they act? Moses recorded his prayer about this specific topic, and we can read it in Deuteronomy 3:24,

O Sovereign Lord, you have only begun to show your greatness and the strength of your hand to me, your

servant. Is there any god in heaven or on earth who can perform such great and mighty deeds as you do?

Is there any god in heaven or on earth, Moses wondered. Well, I guess he knew the answer. He had received the Ten Commandments first-hand from God and number one makes it clear: 'You shall have no other gods before Me.' If we would freely translate or interpret that first commandment, it would come down to this: 'Don't compromise!' or, as I wrote in chapter one: 'it's me or nothing.' That makes it quite clear, doesn't it?

Reading throughout the ancient scriptures we may notice that idol worship was rampant, despite the warnings, under several leaders and kings, but not under all. David, for example, may have done several things wrong, but he never worshiped other gods. The issue of having other gods before our Lord didn't just occur in Old Testament times. Idolatry, as I wrote in my books 'True Worshipers' and 'First Love', was an issue back then and still is just as much an issue today. Let us jump forward for a moment and well to 1 Corinthians 8:5-6, where the apostle Paul wrote:

Even if there are so-called "gods," whether in heaven or on earth, and even though there are many of these "gods" and "lords," yet there is for us only one God, the Father, who is the Creator of all things and for whom we live; and there is only one Lord, Jesus Christ, through whom all things were created and through whom we live.

I believe he answers the question that Moses had. There are many of these gods… in heaven and on earth. It was so during the time of Moses, it was so during the time of Paul, and it is still so in the times we live in today. And it will probably be so until Jesus comes back in full glory.

Other gods compete for the worship we as human beings should bring to the Lord. Satan has always done his best to distract people from their loyalty to God by presenting other gods before them and he is still busy doing so. Anything, anyone, as long as he succeeds in distracting people and keeping them from seeing God for whom He really is: a good God and a loving Father. Worthy of our praise, worthy of our time and devotion.

Meditate on the following:

- *Can I think of any other gods that take away from my devotion to the Lord?*
- *What has God done for me recently?*

Journal your thoughts:

6

He is true

This must be a magnificent Temple because our God is greater than all other gods.

2 Chronicles 2:5 (NLT)

Profoundly sweating and nearly out of breath, we came to the top of a mountain where a small temple had been built by an ancient Inca tribe. Being from a wet and cold country where the weather is highly influenced by the wind and the sea, it takes time to get used to a tropical climate.

The Netherlands, where we live, is a country as flat as a pancake. No mountains, no jungle, no ravines or deserts. Just grasslands, rivers and dunes. And oh yeah, most of it below sea level. There couldn't be a greater contrast with the jungles, mountains, deserts, and valleys of South America. During the first few weeks we were there, we had to find a new rhythm, a new balance. Walk slower, eat less, sleep more, rest at midday, and so forth.

Anyway, during this particular trip we set out to visit one of the many ancient temples or what was left of it. Such temple ruins are places where the ancient gods and their statutes were worshiped. Today, most mystical Inca statues can be found in museums and quite an array of replica's are being offered as souvenirs to tourists. The grim faces of these figures don't make for a friendly welcome. Most of the images of Inca gods have square, symmetric features and kind of a gloomy look. At first they appear kind of funny, but when you study them up close the anger gets to you somehow.

The Inca people left no written records and their legends are often rather mythical than factual. Several Inca temples and ruins have been excavated and somewhat restored, such as the one we visited during our travels. The Inca established their capital at Cuzco in Peru in the 12th century. Cuzco is still an amazing city to visit by the way. The Inca mythology is mainly based on and inspired by nature and acknowledges gods of the sun and moon, earth and the seas. Today there are still descendants of Inca tribes living in the Andes Mountains and they often practice a religion that is a mix of Animism, Catholicism, and cultural practices. They preserve the traditions and continue to worship the Inca gods. You may wonder whether prayers offered to lifeless gods ever get answered?

We know from the ancient biblical story about the Baal gods that the gods remained silent, even when the people fervently prayed and screamed to be heard. We can read that in 1 Kings chapter 18. The prophet Elijah confronted the people with their idolatry. He ordered all the people of Israel to meet at Mount Carmel and to bring along the four hundred and fifty prophets of Baal and the four hundred prophets of the goddess Asherah who were supported by Queen Jezebel. Verse 21 says:

Elijah went up to the people and said, "How much longer will it take you to make up your minds? If the Lord is God, worship him; but if Baal is God, worship him!" But the people didn't say a word.

In essence, he was saying 'Stop your divided loyalty!' and he then challenged the people to bring two bulls and let the prophets of Baal take one, kill it, cut it in pieces, and put it on the wood without lighting the fire. He himself would do the same with the other bull. The prophets of Baal were invited to pray to their god and Elijah to the Lord. The one who would answer by sending fire would be the one and true God. And so it happened. The prophets of Baal prepared the bull and prayed to Baal until noon. Note verse 26,

They shouted, "Answer us, Baal!" and kept dancing around the altar they had built. But no answer came.

But no answer came. How sad, how tragic. At noon Elijah started making fun of them: 'Pray louder!' So the prophets prayed louder and cut themselves with knives and daggers, according to their ritual, until blood flowed.

My goodness, when I think about the amount of young people that cut themselves today until blood flows, it is quite clear that dark forces are behind such practices. It dates back to an ancient Baal worship ritual where people cried out for attention in a desperate quest to be seen and heard

The flowing of blood in itself is a practice quite often mentioned in the Old Testament. As a matter of fact, blood *had* to flow for the forgiveness of sins. Animal blood that was. This practice of animal sacrifices remained into effect until the sacrificial death of Jesus on the cross. He took the sins of the whole world upon Himself, He was the perfect sacrifice, that is why He is also called the Lamb of God. No more killing, no more animal (or human) sacrifices. The Bible makes that very clear.

How heartbreaking it is then to see that followers of many religions today still believe that blood has to flow in order to please the gods. I remember many years ago we found ourselves in the capital of Nepal, Kathmandu. We happened to be there during the Hindu festival of Dashain. In the center of the city animal offerings were being made: goats, ducks, buffalos even, were slaughtered on the altars in the temples. Blood flowed everywhere and it was quite a horrible site to see for us westerners. I remember thinking that in reality their offerings must have been somewhat like the offerings we can read about in the Old Testament. Animal sacrifices and altars splattered with their blood.

Yes, blood had to flow in ancient times, but Jesus drew the line between BC and AD when He shed His precious blood for the forgiveness of the sins of all mankind. Yes, also for the Hindu. This is the truth we need to stand up for today! We must stand up for Jesus and His redemptive work on the cross in order to annul the deceptive beliefs that we can please God or gods by offering blood sacrifices. Truth is a core value for us believers. I wrote about that in my book 'Spirit of Truth.'

Actually, any religion (including satanism) that does *not* acknowledge the suffering of Jesus Christ on the cross, is still bound to occult practices that offer no redemption. We can see that throughout history, we can see it in different cults and religions, and we can still see so today. Blood sacrifices in abortions, in mass killings, in satanic rituals, in religious practices etc. etc.

Let's go back to the story of Elijah and the Baal priests. 1 Kings 18:29 says:

They kept on ranting and raving until the middle of the afternoon; but no answer came, not a sound was heard.

It is really an interesting story, read the whole chapter if you like. Baal worshipers desperately seeking a sign of life, but none came. Not a sound was heard no matter how loud they screamed to be heard. And then it was God's turn. Elijah's prayer was simple. He asked God to prove Himself to be the one true God, supreme over all other gods. You will find out that the God of Elijah answered his prayer in a spectacular way with fire from heaven that ignited the altar Elijah had drenched with water. In verses 38-39 it is described like this,

The Lord sent fire down, and it burned up the sacrifice, the wood, and the stones, scorched the earth and dried up the water in the trench. When the people saw this, they threw themselves on the ground and exclaimed, "The Lord is God; the Lord alone is God!"

It was quite a showdown and I truly believe such stories are in the Bible as a lesson for all of us, for all generations. The ones that were, the ones that are now, and the ones still to come. There is in reality one God who is supreme over all other gods. He is the Creator of the universe, the Maker of heaven and earth, the God of Israel.

He is the One who answers our prayers, who delights in answering our prayers. We don't have to yell and scream or cut ourselves to be heard, to arouse the attention of our heavenly Father who loved us from the beginning of time. We can simply come before Him with our requests and wait expectantly, as Psalm 5:3 (NIV) so beautifully describes,

*In the morning, Lord, you hear my voice; in the morning
I lay my requests before you and wait expectantly.*

Our heavenly Father, who did not even keep his own Son
from us, cannot be compared with any other god. He
alone deserves our worship, He alone is worthy of our
praise. His face isn't grim, His face is shining down upon
us and He gives us peace.

Meditate on the following:

- *What can I thank my heavenly Father for, today?*
- *Can I say that I wait expectantly for my prayers to be answered?*

Journal your thoughts:

7

He is honorable

The Lord is great and is to be highly praised; he is to be honored more than all the gods. The gods of all other nations are only idols, but the Lord created the heavens.

Psalm 96:4-5

Although traveling all over the world taught us that every region or nation has its own culture, customs, and religious practices, we also discovered that certain biblical ideas and principles can be found everywhere. And not only so because people have read the Bible in their own language. Some biblical stories are interwoven in the historical and cultural accounts of other religions.

The story of Adam and Eve in the garden, as we know it from the account in the book of Genesis, can be found as part of various other religious works and cultural legends. The story differs in details, but the main points are the same. This is also true for the account of Noah and the great flood. Many such similar accounts can be found in other religious writings and in that sense they all have historical oral traditions in common.

I remember many years ago when we were visiting the Navajo nation in western United States. We learned there that most indigenous people in Canada and the United States believe there is one Great Spirit among other spirits. Just in the same way as we acknowledge the Holy Spirit, who is God, as well as spirits with a small s. Lesser spirits or demons, such as a spirit of infirmity, a spirit of fear, or an unclean spirit. Native Americans are traditionally very spiritual people, and most tribes revere the Great Spirit, which is basically an English translation for the creator, a deity or god.

Acknowledging God the Creator of heaven and earth is one thing, I am sure the ancient Israelites did just that. But staying away from other 'lesser' gods is another thing. Now, we may wonder what was so attractive about other gods that the ancient Israelites were constantly enticed into worshiping them? We have already established the fact that there *are* other gods, otherwise the first commandment would lose its value. But we have also seen that those other gods were not and are not real. There is no life in statues, there is no love in idols, there is no breath in pictures.

In his letter to the Galatians, the apostle Paul voiced his concern about the dangers of worshiping other gods. He wrote:

In the past you did not know God, and so you were slaves of beings who are not gods (Galatians 4:8).

The NKJV says: 'But then, indeed, when you did not know God, you served those which by nature are not gods.' In other words, the people regarded their idols as gods and called them gods, but by nature they were not. What is the nature of God, we might ask. His nature is eternally good, divinely powerful, and forever loving. Now this cannot be said about any god made by human hands.

No matter how beautiful and how costly and how precious a statue may be, there is no life in man-made matter. It is God's nature to forgive, to heal, to deliver, to restore, to love and nurture all that He has created. We can try all we want, but we cannot ascribe the characteristics of a loving heavenly Father to an object made by human hands.

Idols and objects are no gods at all, however there are demons attached to such objects. No, I am not making that up, the Bible teaches it. And I believe that is why the so-called other gods are dangerous. Just as much as the Holy Spirit needs a human body to operate through here on earth, demons need a body to operate through here on earth. This is exactly why having statues of foreign gods in your home is dangerous. The statue cannot do anything of course, but dark forces come with the statue and gain entrance into your home. The statue is an official invitation for the enemy to be present.

The Bible is clear about the idols, they can do nothing. But the demons behind the idols, they wreak havoc wherever they can. The apostle Paul wrote about such dark forces in quite direct words:

For we are not fighting against human beings but against the wicked spiritual forces in the heavenly world, the rulers, authorities, and cosmic powers of this dark age (Ephesians 6:12).

No, I am not seeing a demon behind every tree or building, don't get me wrong. But I truly believe Christians are often too ignorant when it comes to everything happening in the spiritual realm. Remember Paul's words 'don't be ignorant'? Well, let's therefore take a look at 1 Corinthians 10:18-21, where the apostle Paul writes,

Consider the people of Israel; those who eat what is offered in sacrifice share in the altar's service to God. Do I imply, then, that an idol or the food offered to it really amounts to anything? No! What I am saying is that what is sacrificed on pagan altars is offered to demons, not to God. And I do not want you to be partners with demons.

An idol doesn't amount to anything, Paul writes, but it is the demons that we should shy away from. Do not partner with demons! Well, who wants to partner with demons, you might wonder? Just take a look around you in our current society, millions of people are slaves to demons while, in reality, they could be sons and daughters of God.

If you have ever been involved in praying for people who are being tormented by demons, you know this is real. Demons gain entrance to our bodies through occult practices, sexual immorality, through associating with demons, partnering with demons, just as Paul wrote. I guess it was daily practice in Corinth, because he mentions it as a matter of fact. 1 Corinthians 10:21 says,

You cannot drink the cup of the Lord and the cup of demons; you cannot partake of the Lord's table and of the table of demons.

Basically, Paul is saying that we should not mix the evils of the world with our religious practices. We cannot serve both God and Mammon. We cannot serve two masters, we will love the one and hate the other. We must choose, each day, between good and evil, between God and the world, between life and death.

I strongly believe that the first commandment holds a solid warning, not to make our lives difficult, but to make it easier. You shall have no other gods before me… obeying those words would make life better, more focused, less fearful, less dramatic. I truly believe the first commandment is tied to the greatest commandment as Jesus cited it in Matthew 22:37-38 (NIV), when the people asked Him what the greatest commandment was.

Jesus replied: "'Love the Lord your God with all your heart and with all your soul and with all your mind.' This is the first and greatest commandment."

In light of the view I have taken in this book series, I believe Jesus gave them the fulfillment of the letter of the first commandment. It's one thing to say you have no other gods before Him, it's another thing to love Him above all else! Do you see why Jesus did that?

He did so with all the commandments. In the second half of Matthew chapter 5, we can read that Jesus reminded the crowd over and over that it was said: 'You shall not do this or that'. And then He added: 'But now I tell you….' and He gave them an inside out, upside down version of the Law. He left the people speechless, all the time. He is still leaving people speechless today. The Law has not disappeared, but we are called to fulfill the commandments in love. Every time we act in love, we fulfill the Law. Romans 13:10 says it clearly:

Love is the fulfillment of the Law.

If we say we cannot fulfill the Law, we are basically saying that we are unable to love. Well, in a world that denies Christ and thus is full of hatred, it certainly turns out to be that way. And this is exactly the reason why Jesus continued His answer with the following statement:

And the second is like it: 'Love your neighbor as yourself.' All the Law and the Prophets hang on these two commandments (Matthew 22:39-40 , NIV).

The Law and the prophets hang on these two commandments. The commandments to love God and others as ourselves. Hold on a minute, you might think. The Law is about obedience, right? And disobedience is punishable. No! Jesus says the drive, the fundamental basics or the main core value of Christianity is love. Now, that puts the commandments in a totally different light, doesn't it?

If you have read any of the previous books in this series, you know what I am talking about. If you have read any of the previous books, you know that our lives are to be lived in the light of His unending love. Now, that would make this world a better place already.

Meditate on the following:

- *Can I say I am loyal, undivided when it comes to loving and serving God?*
- *Trying to serve two masters, do I see it in my own life?*

Journal your thoughts:

8

He is eternal

Has a nation changed its gods,

Which are not gods?

But My people have changed their Glory

For what does not profit.

Jeremiah 2:11 (NKJV)

We took one of those longboats to travel to our destination. Longboats are a favorite and fast means of transportation in Thailand. The small boats move forward like sharks cutting through the water, a huge power engine pushing full speed ahead.

The journey took us to a temple with an astonishing amount of Buddha statues. Tourists swarmed the site, taking as many pictures as possible of the statues covered in gold. Quite a sight, I must admit. During our many travels we came across a great diversity of cultures and religions. It made us realize how small our own world, being from a tiny country like the Netherlands, really was.

Growing up in a Christian family, we had no dealings with other religions, except Judaism maybe. So, to see great masses of people worshiping, bowing down to shiny statues covered with gold and fabrics was rather strange to us. No matter what the people did, the statues never moved, never blinked an eye, and never smiled. There was always this coldness, this distance.

Now, it is clear from all the stories we can read in the Bible, that each nation had their god or gods, just as Israel had the Lord Yahweh as their God. Micah 4:5 reveals,

Each nation worships and obeys its own god, but we will worship and obey the Lord our God forever and ever.

I am not a theologian and I am not sure whether God assigned each nation a god or whether they picked their own. What matters is that He chose Israel as His own and later on adopted us gentiles as His children as well, a great privilege. Every person on the face of the earth has been created with a free will which we can use to accept or reject Him as Lord. Acts 14:16 even says that in the past, He let all nations go their own way. No one ever gets pressured into believing that He is the one and true God. In one way or another each person needs to go on his or her own quest to find out whether He really is who He says He is.

It has been like this for thousands of years, we can read the historical events in the Bible. Every now and then a showdown took place (as was the case with Elisha and the Baal priests, as we read in chapter 6) and God even challenged these so-called other gods. Isaiah described such a happening in chapter 41. Let's take a look at verses 21-23 where it is written:

The Lord, the king of Israel, has this to say: "You gods of the nations, present your case. Bring the best arguments you have! Come here and predict what will happen, so that we will know it when it takes place. Explain to the court the events of the past, and tell us what they mean. Tell us what the future holds—then we will know that you are gods!"

Present your case! God is calling the gods of the nations to come and prove that they are truly gods. Can you believe that? He challenges them and gives them a chance to prove their power. Nothing happens. Silence. Coldness and frozen looks. God's conclusion should be a lesson for all of us, no matter where we are in life. Don't put your trust in lifeless idols. Never! Just read the words of the Lord in verses 28 and 29:

When I looked among the gods, none of them had a thing to say; not one could answer the questions I asked. All these gods are useless; they can do nothing at all—these idols are weak and powerless.

None of them had a thing to say. That sentence intrigues me. The God of the Bible is a God who speaks. He speaks through His Word, He speaks through His Holy Spirit, and He speaks to people personally, such as was the case when I heard Him speak about writing this book series. God created the heavens and the earth by His words. His words have the power to create, to heal, to restore, and to encourage. I love how it is written (yeah, words again) in Hebrews 1:1-3,

Long ago God spoke many times and in many ways to our ancestors through the prophets. And now in these final days, he has spoken to us through his Son. God promised everything to the Son as an inheritance, and through the Son he created the universe. The Son radiates God's own glory and expresses the very character of God, and he sustains everything by the mighty power of his command.

We serve a speaking God, not one who remains silent, although there might be seasons in our lives when it seems He is silent. When we go through such periods of spiritual dryness we still have His written Word. God has spoken to us through His Son and many of these words have been recorded for our benefit.

Anyway, 'none of them had a thing to say.' Was God disappointed? No, I don't think so. He merely wanted to prove a point, for the Israelites to see, as well as for future generations. When we continue reading in Isaiah chapter 42 where God introduces the coming Messiah, His one and only Son, He said (verses 8 and 9):

I alone am the Lord your God. No other god may share my glory; I will not let idols share my praise. The things I predicted have now come true. Now I will tell you of new things even before they begin to happen.

He made it clear, yes, there are so-called other gods. But they do not have the power God has and they cannot and will not share in His glory. And then He ends by saying that He is the God who can predict the future, who knows what is going to happen even before it has begun. Simply because He is eternal. He is not bound by time or place. He knows the beginning from the end, which is quite a comfort once you believe that He is a good God and a loving Father.

It is truly my hope and prayer that we gain wisdom by going through these ancient scriptures. If there is anything we need in the times we live in, it is wisdom. Wisdom is another core value for believers. We go after so many worldly things nowadays, while in reality we are called to desire spiritual virtues such as wisdom. I wrote extensively about that in my book 'My Neighbor's House.' We need wisdom in order to keep standing in a world full of foolishness.

Even if you remember only one thing from this book, let it be that other gods amount to nothing, but demons can wreak havoc. Demons are real, whether we believe so or not. Demons did not cease to exist under the new covenant. About Jesus it is written that He traveled all over Galilee, preaching in the synagogues and driving out demons. The apostle Paul warned Timothy that some people would abandon the faith in later times by obeying lying spirits and following the teachings of demons.

And then of course there is the battle of the end times. In Revelation 9:20 it is written,

The rest of the human race, all those who had not been killed by these plagues, did not turn away from what they themselves had made. They did not stop worshiping demons, nor the idols of gold, silver, bronze, stone, and wood, which cannot see, hear, or walk.

A time has been predicted in the Bible where people will not stop worshiping demons. Could that time be now? We might not do so on purpose, but when our loyalty towards God is divided we give room to demons and that should not be so.

Meditate on the following:

- *Have I ever experienced God's power at work in my life through the Word?*
- *The Word of God is…*

Journal your thoughts:

9

He is loving

Give thanks to the Lord, because he is good; his love is eternal. Give thanks to the greatest of all gods; his love is eternal. Give thanks to the mightiest of all lords; his love is eternal.

Psalm 136:1-3

One of the most spectacular temple complexes we ever visited during our years of traveling was Abu Simbel In Egypt. The rock-cut temple was dedicated to several ancient gods as well as to King Ramses himself. It is generally considered the grandest and most beautiful of the temples commissioned during the reign of Ramses II, and one of the most beautiful in Egypt.

Although it is an adventure to walk around this site and step back in time, something feels odd, kind of spooky even. There is no life, no music, no friendship or family gathering. Not even prayer. Again, there is silence and coldness. In that sense the site is not attractive. I remember that we walked away from the complex with a feeling of sadness.

Looking back I wonder if maybe that was because we did not find what we were looking for at the time. We were not practicing believers back then but we never really stopped looking for signs that the God of the Bible we grew up with was real. That He still touched people and that He still performed miracles. We longed for some form of spirituality that would fulfill us.

In that sense, I believe many (young) travelers are seekers. Seekers for truth, for adventure, for a genuine encounter with a god maybe. They can be found all over the world, visiting ancient temples and burial sites, sometimes even joining certain religious groups or cults. Backpacking, certainly back then, was often a pilgrimage in disguise. We visited our share of religious and cultural heritage sites out of historical and anthropological interest but certainly also out of curiosity and a longing for spiritual connection. And although archaeologically speaking these sites are important and impressive… there is no spirituality there. God is not among the other gods, who are all dead. He is the God of the living. He breathes, He loves, He forgives, He shines and warms our hearts, if we let Him.

Man-made gods are not really gods, they are mere idols. Let's take a look at 1 Corinthians 8:4-6 where the apostle Paul writes,

So then, about eating the food offered to idols: we know that an idol stands for something that does not really exist; we know that there is only the one God. Even if there are so-called "gods," whether in heaven or on earth, and even though there are many of these "gods" and "lords," yet there is for us only one God, the Father, who is the Creator of all things and for whom we live; and there is only one Lord, Jesus Christ, through whom all things were created and through whom we live.

As we have already seen throughout this book, yes, there are other gods, and no, they are not real. The demons behind them, however, are very real. In ancient times, whatever was sacrificed on pagan altars, was not sacrificed to God but to demons. I can't say whether the people involved realized that at the time. It is my guess that they didn't. Who wants to offer sacrifices to demons? You would have to be out of your mind to willingly be involved in demon worship.

Personally, I believe that the people just did what they saw their ancestors doing and didn't give it much thought. It wasn't until Paul came and preached the Gospel to them that their eyes were opened for the Truth. Nowadays, a lack of biblical knowledge as well as a lack of knowledge about the spiritual world and the true nature of occult practices lures people into dangerous situations. Someone has to share the Gospel to put these practices in proper perspective. You can ask any

Christian who came out of occult practices and they will confirm that the truth has set them free!

The gods that are no gods at all are no match for the Great I Am who is the only true God. The reality is that there are other gods, but the truth is that there is only one God who is alive and who has all the power and glory and dominion for ever and ever. God Himself made it clear, as we can read in Deuteronomy 31:19,

With their idols they have made me angry, jealous with their so-called gods, gods that are really not gods.

Gods that are not really gods, yet the worship of such gods made Him angry and jealous. It is almost like opposites are colliding here. Other gods are not really gods, yet they are in some way. I think Paul understood it, he must have gained insight reading through the old scrolls while looking at the contemporary society around him (in Israel and in Greece). He wrote: 'even if there are so-called gods…' I think we agreed on that as well, there *are* other gods, otherwise the first commandment would be of no use. Maybe he recognized the danger of religious activities without a personal encounter with God Himself. Just joining rituals because everyone is doing it.

Paul (his name was still Saul at the time) even approved the killing of Stephen at a time the church in Jerusalem suffered terribly and he made a lot of trouble for the church. He went from house to house, arresting men and women and putting them in jail. You can read all of that in Acts 8. Man, was he ever deceived and blind to the truth. When he came to faith, he realized all the mistakes he had made in the name of religion and he took his task of warning others for that danger very seriously. Misdirected ideological zeal can lead to murder, remember that. We can see it in many terrorist actions today.

Paul also understood the danger of denying the existence of so-called gods, or more precisely, idols. He warned sternly against the worship of idols and against eating food offered to idols. Let's take a look again at the eye-opening passage in 1 Corinthians 10:18-21,

Consider the people of Israel; those who eat what is offered in sacrifice share in the altar's service to God. Do I imply, then, that an idol or the food offered to it really amounts to anything? No! What I am saying is that what is sacrificed on pagan altars is offered to demons, not to God. And I do not want you to be partners with demons. You cannot drink from the Lord's cup and also from the cup of demons; you cannot eat at the Lord's table and also at the table of demons. Or do we want to make the Lord jealous? Do we think that we are stronger than he?

What is sacrificed on pagan altars is offered to demons. So maybe the so-called gods are not real, but the demons are. I think we can see this clearly today. People might not be literally bowing down to a statue, but they are sacrificing human lives to the demon of abortion. That brings me to another core value for believers: Protection of life. Life is a God-given gift and all of life is precious to God, whether that is life of the unborn, the disabled, the elderly or the rejected. If you have never read my book 'Breath of Life', I recommend you to do so. It truly deals with the sanctity of life.

So, as I wrote, people might not be literally bowing down to a statue, but they are sacrificing their money, health, and future to the demon of addiction. They are sacrificing their integrity to the demon of greed and deception and they are sacrificing their purity to the demons of sexual perversity, lust, and pornography. Yeah, in that sense the danger is enormous.

Of course there is nothing new under the sun. We can read in Deuteronomy 32:16-17 (NLT) how Israel aroused the jealousy of God by worshiping other gods, and thus demons,

They stirred up his jealousy by worshiping foreign gods; they provoked his fury with detestable deeds. They offered sacrifices to demons, which are not God, to gods they had not known before, to new gods only recently arrived, to gods their ancestors had never feared.

In his eye-opening passage in 1 Corinthians 10:18-21 Paul must have referred to the sacrificing to demons as mentioned here in Deuteronomy. Now why in the world would anyone in his or her right mind sacrifice to demons? What would be the benefit, what would be the result? The Bible says that when we worship God, He inhabits our praises. In other words, He is very near when we worship Him. His presence is tangible when we worship Him. We become like the one we worship. Now, if that works the same with worshiping demons, just try to imagine what kind of fear, destruction, and havoc is being created by the worshiping of demons. No wonder the first commandment says: 'Have no other gods before Me'.

We have the promise of God though, that He will reduce the gods of the earth to nothing, and then every nation will worship Him, each in its own land (Zephaniah 2:11). That tells me the so-called gods must be removed, maybe even more than that… they will have to admit that there is only one God. The psalmist understood it and looked forward to that moment. Psalm 97:6-7,

The heavens proclaim his righteousness, and all the nations see his glory. Everyone who worships idols is put to shame; all the gods bow down before the Lord.

What a sight that will be. The gods bowing down, the demons trembling before the Lord, before the Lord of glory. And the ones who worshiped idols will be put to shame, simply because they will see that the so-called gods they had been running after amount to nothing. It could be greed, lust, pride, power, praise from people, education, or elitism. It will all amount to nothing when God reveals His glory and His supremacy over all other things on earth, in heaven and under the earth.

Whether people believe this or not, that moment will come. It is highly recommended to prepare ourselves, to make sure we are not, in any way or form, serving other gods. Serving other gods results in being harassed by the demons behind them. The spiritual realm may still hold many secrets for us, but the Bible makes it clear that spiritual powers, evil forces, and principalities are present and very active.

However and whenever, the day will surely come for the gods to bow down. And we will sing:

I thank you, Lord, with all my heart; I sing praise to you before the gods (Psalm 138:1).

I believe that will be a glorious moment, a moment of triumph when all eyes will see, and all minds will grasp, and all hearts will love the One who is above it all!

Meditate on the following:

- *Demons. What comes to mind?*
- *Do I worship/revere anyone or anything besides God?*

Journal your thoughts:

10

He is forgiving

The Lord is great and is to be highly praised; he is to be honored more than all the gods.

1 Chronicles 16:25

We found ourselves in a small town in Bolivia, high up in the Andes Mountains, during the annual Carnival festivities. It seemed to be the highlight of the year, everyone was so excited!

Each day another procession came through the small and windy streets of the town we were staying in. The people were dressed in colorful attire, many of them drunk with local brews, while carrying statues and images of the various saints derived from a mix of Catholicism and indigenous religions. The crowds danced and slowly moved uphill to the nearest church where other rituals took place, unknown to us people from Western Europe.

During the Carnival festivities in Bolivia we avoided entering local churches, simply because there were too many people and there was too much noise. We just couldn't see how any of the rituals performed had anything to do with true religion, whatever the concept was we had back then. The people were rowdy but not joyful, they were loud but not really on fire, they were singing but not praising. It was an outward form of religion, but it lacked real power.

All throughout the ages we have seen that people wanted a god they could see and touch. A god that they could visit, bow down to, and move from place to place. The desire for a god that can be seen, heard, felt, and touched is understandable and at the same time unrealistic. The desire for a god that is like humans leads to the making of images and statues and ultimately leads to idolatry... the worship of man-made things. The Bible describes it exactly the other way around: God desires people to be like Himself.

Our lack of spiritual understanding often keeps us trapped in human thinking. It happened to the ancient Israelites. They seriously and desperately asked one of their leaders, Aaron:

Make us gods who will go before us. As for this fellow Moses who brought us up out of Egypt, we don't know what has happened to him (Exodus 32:23, NIV).

The crazy thing was that they *had* a god who went before them in a pillar of fire by night and a cloud by day. They had a god who showed Himself to be real by traveling ahead of them with visible and tangible signs. But somehow they began to think that it was not enough. They wanted someone they could see, they could bow down to. We see this desire to make God fit into our human mind coming back in Christianity as well as in most other religions. We see it coming back all the time in the desire to worship man-made idols, symbols, statues, paintings, memorabilia, etc. etc. instead of the One who made everything, the One who spoke the Word and it all came into being.

Of course the human desire to see and touch God came as no surprise to our heavenly Father. He gave us the very best and most exact representation of Himself in His Son Jesus Christ, who came to earth as a man to live among the people and show them the true character of the God they could not see. Hebrews 1:3 (NLT) says it beautifully,

The Son radiates God's own glory and expresses the very character of God, and he sustains everything by the mighty power of his command.

Jesus expresses the very character of God. Think about that. Everything the people saw in Him, and everything that was written down for us to read about Him, expresses the very character of God. Who says we cannot know God? Who says He is a faraway God that remains mysterious? Jesus made Him known, He was God among us, Immanuel. Jesus gave a face to God. He lived here on earth and walked among us. He showed us the way to stay connected by giving us His Holy Spirit who would remain with us until the end of time. The Holy Spirit produces godly character in believers: love, mercy, kindness, patience, fairness, justice, grace, joy, peace, and self-control… Character traits that will make God visible in us! Acts 17:29-30 says,

Since we are God's children, we should not suppose that his nature is anything like an image of gold or silver or stone, shaped by human art and skill. God has overlooked the times when people did not know him, but now he commands all of them everywhere to turn away from their evil ways.

Forget the images and statues. We have a God that can be seen, that can be felt, and that can be experienced, now more than ever because He sent us the Holy Spirit. The Spirit of Truth who was poured out on us in order that He could bring glory to Jesus and whisper secrets from the Father's heart to us. How awesome is that? Why would we run after man-made matters instead of running after Him, who is Spirit, to get to know Him better?

Why do we spend so much time getting to know everything the world has to offer and so little time exploring His powerful Word that sustains the whole universe? Jesus is the living Word of God, it was His desire to bring glory to the Father by making Him known, by granting the prayer requests we send up to God. He does not want to remain a mystery. As a matter of fact, He gave gifts to the church, the body of believers, so that we can come to a full knowledge of the Son of God. This is the God we serve. He is real, He is all-knowing and all-powerful. He is all-present and forever loving. No idol, no other god can ever stand in His shadow and remain standing. No other god possesses the attributes the God of Israel has. No statue has ever shown love or extended mercy. No statue has ever healed the sick or opened the eyes of the blind. No statue has ever shown generosity.

The God of the Bible is generous, so generous that He gave His only beloved Son to rescue the world from darkness, destruction, and death. His Son came to earth to give us life, a life in all its fullness. This is in stark contrast with the works of Satan and his demons. He comes only to steal, kill, and destroy. He is a thief. Jesus is a giver! Generosity, therefore, is a core value for believers. My award winning book 'Grace of Giving' deals with the works of the thief and the works of Jesus. Don't miss out!

In His generosity, Jesus did what no statue has ever been able to do and that is to forgive our sins and wipe away our tears of shame and guilt. No statue has ever been able to grant us a brand new beginning. Jesus is able. 2 Corinthians 5:17 makes it clear:

Anyone who is joined to Christ is a new being; the old is gone, the new has come.

Meditate on the following:

- *What is my relationship with the Holy Spirit like?*
- *How do I spend time with Him?*

Journal your thoughts:

11

He is great

I know that our Lord is great, greater than all the gods.

Psalm 135:5

One of the joys of traveling to different lands and getting to know different cultures is the introduction to languages. During our extensive travels throughout Mexico, Central and South America we signed up for a Spanish language course in Antigua, Guatemala, and learned quite a bit. Well, at least enough to make small talk and ask some questions.

Although modern-day Spanish is very useful in the regions as mentioned above, it is not very helpful when trying to decipher ancient languages such as the Aztec language. The Aztecs were the Native American people who dominated northern Mexico at the time of the Spanish conquest in the early 16th century. Although originally a nomadic culture, the Aztecs eventually settled on several small islands in Lake Texcoco where they founded the town of Tenochtitlan, modern-day Mexico City.

We visited several museums that were dedicated to Aztec culture and I remember being horrified by the idea that they would rip out human hearts, beating hearts believe it or not, to offer them to their sun gods and goddesses. These gods had names quite hard to pronounce, such as Huitzilopochtli, Quetzalcoatl, and Tezcatlipoca. Well, so much for trying to learn Spanish.

As we have seen in many other cultures and ancient religions, the gods were gods of war and battle. Their characters vicious, angry, and often violent. There is no statue, no idol, nor ancient god or goddess with the ability to extend love or to guide people into safety. We know from biblical history that that is exactly how God showed Himself to be true over and over again, for example in the Book of Joshua. When Joshua asked the people whom they would serve, God or other gods, their answer was clear as we can read in chapter 24:16-17:

The people replied, "We would never leave the Lord to serve other gods! The Lord our God brought our fathers and us out of slavery in Egypt, and we saw the miracles that he performed. He kept us safe wherever we went among all the nations through which we passed."

'He kept us safe', well, that is more than enough to give God glory. The people acknowledged that God had been watching over them all the time and they promised to never abandon Him and to faithfully serve Him. Verse 31 of that same chapter says,

As long as Joshua lived, the people of Israel served the Lord, and after his death they continued to do so as long as those leaders were alive who had seen for themselves everything that the Lord had done for Israel.

They continued to serve God as long as the leaders were alive that witnessed the miracles. One generation, that is how long the memory was kept alive which was enough to keep the people close to God. We know from the rest of the story however, that they did turn to other gods later on. We can read in Judges 2:10,

That whole generation also died, and the next generation forgot the Lord and what he had done for Israel.

Oh my goodness, if this doesn't show the importance of remembrance, I don't know what will. It is crucial that we tell our children and our children's children what the Lord has done for us. Simply, because they need to know what a great God He is. If we don't testify, if we keep silent, the next generation will be led astray by other people raising their voices and celebrating their pride and victories.

The people of Israel forgot the Lord! How is it possible? They stopped worshiping the Lord, the God of their ancestors, the God who had brought them out of Egypt, and they began to worship other gods, the gods of the peoples around them. They bowed down to them and made the Lord angry. Read Judges 2 and see for yourself how their decisions led to disaster. The Lord became so furious with Israel that He let raiders attack and rob them. He let the enemies all around overpower them, and the Israelites could no longer protect themselves.

'He kept us safe', more than enough to give God glory. Remember that? A generation after that, they found themselves without protection because they had turned to worthless idols. Because they had put their trust in man-made gods that were not gods at all. So-called gods that were cold and lifeless, and so were the demons behind them. Instead of bringing life they brought death and destruction on various levels.

In essence, all demons are anti-God, and so they are against everything the Creator of heaven and earth stands for. Think life, love, light, forgiveness, grace, patience, mercy, joy, abundance, restoration, rest, and renewal. If you can find any of these divine attributes in the occult, tell me. It would truly surprise me.

Is there any god who prescribes rest for his people? Let's be honest here, the gods of this world have people running around, living frenzy lives, lacking peace. I know people who are into mindfulness, eastern meditation, and such New Age practices. They are desperately seeking peace, but are unable to find it. God, however, gives us true peace as well as a clear recipe for staying happy and healthy: a day of rest after every six days of work. Regular rest is a core value for every believer! Check out my book 'Sacred Sabbath', which is the first book in this series of ten.

The other gods are quite accurately described in Psalm 115:2-8,

Why should the nations ask us, "Where is your God?" Our God is in heaven; he does whatever he wishes. Their gods are made of silver and gold, formed by human hands. They have mouths, but cannot speak, and eyes, but cannot see. They have ears, but cannot hear, and noses, but cannot smell. They have hands, but cannot feel, and feet, but cannot walk; they cannot make a sound. May all who made them and who trust in them become like the idols they have made.

Now, that is quite a serious warning, to become like the idols we make: lifeless, deaf, mute, immovable. Basically, not being able to do anything at all, going down with the idols to the land of the dead.

It has always amazed me that certain cultures and kingdoms seem to have vanished from the earth. The ancient Egyptians, the Mayans, the Incas, the Aztecs, their civilizations are no longer existent. I wonder if they became like the idols they trusted and vanished from the earth.

Meditate on the following:

- *Write down several things God has done in my life.*

- *Have I ever made promises to God that I did not keep?*

Journal your thoughts:

12

I have been the Lord your God ever since I brought you out of Egypt. You must acknowledge no God but me, for there is no other savior.

Hosea 13:4b (NLT)

We stood in awe as we looked up to the Parthenon, the temple that dominates the hill of the Acropolis at Athens. A temple dedicated to the Greek goddess Athena Parthenos. The Parthenon is probably the most famous temple in all of Greece, although the whole country is scattered with temples that were meant to serve as homes for the individual god or goddess who supposedly protected and sustained the community.

The god or goddess was represented by a cult image—usually a seated or standing statue—which occupied the central place in the temple. In the early days they would have been made of wood, but over the years more permanent and costly materials were preferred—stone or cast bronze. I lost track of how many of these ancient sites we visited as well as of most of the names of the Greek gods and goddesses. One thing, however, I remember from the information displayed at temple and museum sites and that is the fact that the gods of Greek mythology were not all necessarily friendly gods. Destructive powers were ascribed to them.

If you've ever read through the whole Old Testament, you may have noticed that the God of Israel wasn't always friendly either. On many occasions He rose in fury against His people because they ran after other gods. He furthermore did not hesitate to bring destruction on their enemies. Although things have changed quite a bit since He sent Jesus to earth, God Himself has not changed. We sometimes made Him to be too sweet and Santa Claus-like if you ask me. Yes, God is love and yes, God is also righteous and He will judge the world with fairness.

We as Christians have often mixed the love of God with our tolerance for disobedience, even within the church. But God does not tolerate evil. Yes, He is patient and kind and yes, we will move away from under His protection when we are disobedient and refuse to acknowledge Him for who He truly is. When we belong to Him, we have nothing to fear, we have nothing to hide, and we have nothing to hold back. However, we should stay away from evil, from sin, from false gods. Please, read 1 John 5:19-21 with me,

We know that we belong to God even though the whole world is under the rule of the Evil One. We know that the Son of God has come and has given us understanding, so that we know the true God. We live in union with the true God—in union with his Son Jesus Christ. This is the true God, and this is eternal life. My children, keep yourselves safe from false gods!

Keep yourselves safe from false gods! This warning comes from the apostle John, the one Jesus loved. The apostle who stood at the foot of the cross. The apostle who wrote one of the gospels which is almost entirely a direct revelation of the teachings and prayers out of the mouth of Jesus. The apostle who wrote three letters about the kind of life believers should live. And yes, the apostle who received apocalyptic insights and wrote the Book of Revelation. He spoke about the one true God because he knew Him, he had been with Him and saw His glory.

He received insight about the spiritual battle that takes place between the devil with his demons and the children of God. He understood as no other that it was no joke and certainly not something to be ignorant about. For sure he was familiar with the old writings of the psalmists, such as in Psalm 16:4 (NLT),

Troubles multiply for those who chase after other gods. I will not take part in their sacrifices of blood or even speak the names of their gods.

Troubles multiply when we chase after other gods. It calls for a thorough introspective look of the lives we are living as Christians. Have we bowed down to the gods of greed, wealth, selfishness, pride, addiction, consumerism, ambition, intellectuality, immorality, and so on, and so on? Let's face the truth here, the devil is *always* looking for someone he *may* devour. We give him access by forsaking our loyalty to God.

The devil even tried his tricks with Jesus, for crying out loud. In Luke 4:5-8 we can read that as follows,

Then the Devil took him up and showed him in a second all the kingdoms of the world. "I will give you all this power and all this wealth," the Devil told him. "It has all been handed over to me, and I can give it to anyone I choose. All this will be yours, then, if you worship me." Jesus answered, "The scripture says, 'Worship the Lord your God and serve only him!'"

The answer Jesus gave him is the only right answer, worship and serve God only. Don't even think about following other gods or idols who cannot be trusted with our very souls. On the contrary, the demons behind the false gods and idols will wreak havoc, bring about much drama, and can cause serious and life-threatening health problems. The Bible gives several examples of people suffering because of evil spirits. These things are real and we must stay far from that.

Nowadays people are very involved with issues such as the weather, climate change, atmospheric happenings etc. So much so that it is turning into a cult, a religion. Yes, even idol worship. As Christians we must be alert and make sure we do not overstep the boundaries God has set. He made it very clear in His Word that the ones who belong to Him must live a different life. Deuteronomy 4:19 says,

Do not be tempted to worship and serve what you see in the sky—the sun, the moon, and the stars. The Lord your God has given these to all other peoples for them to worship.

People are given over to worshiping idols, but the moment a person comes to a saving knowledge of God, things will change. Our interests will change. Our devotion will change. Our loyalty will change.

Deuteronomy 32:4 says that the Lord is our mighty defender, perfect and just in all His ways. He is faithful and true and He does what is right and fair. Now, who wouldn't want to follow such a faithful God? It is good to realize and proclaim over and over again that He is perfect in all of His ways. And the best thing is that He guarantees His protection over our lives. Paul expressed that quite beautifully in Romans 8:38-39,

For I am certain that nothing can separate us from his love: neither death nor life, neither angels nor other

heavenly rulers or powers, neither the present nor the future, neither the world above nor the world below— there is nothing in all creation that will ever be able to separate us from the love of God which is ours through Christ Jesus our Lord.

Meditate on the following:

- *Is there unnecessary drama in my life that I could avoid?*
- *Where do I seek my protection from danger?*

Journal your thoughts:

13

He is light

*People of Israel, you are my witnesses; I chose you to be
my servant, so that you would know me and believe in me
and understand that I am the only God. Besides me there
is no other god; there never was and never will be.*

Isaiah 43:10

One of our very first trips together was with an old
camper van. We were heading towards the north cape,
driving through mountain areas, fjords and tundra lands.
We took our time, the camper was slow and life was
good.

As a matter of fact it was our first trip after my husband
had a terrible motorcycle accident that left him with four
broken vertebras and a broken pelvis and many other
painful things. Anyway, that is another story in itself. But
we took our time, traveling slowly, enjoying the
countryside, which is really spectacular in Norway. We
visited some museums and theme parks on our way and
learned a thing or two about trolls and Scandinavian
mythology.

Troll is a term used to describe various supernatural beings in Nordic folklore and storytelling traditions. These creatures are often both dangerous and stupid. A tourist leaflet at Lillehammer describes trolls as: 'Strong, evil and dangerous giants. Ugly, with large noses and eyes the size of plates, and often with several heads or just one eye. Most lived in the mountains or in a distant, cold country, but trolls living in the ocean or forest also existed.'

In Scandinavian mythology several gods and goddesses are mentioned. Although not in vast numbers as we can see in Hinduism for example, they are still quite known. When I think about the stories about all the gods and goddesses, trolls and strange creatures we have encountered during our travels, it is clear that most of them are described as angry, dark, dangerous, unpredictable, explosive etc. Hardly any friendly or funny ones to be found.

In general people feared the gods, and most of their lives were spent trying to please the gods so they wouldn't curse them. No mythological figure was ever able to love, to extend grace and forgiveness. No so-called god could heal a broken heart or a broken arm for that matter. No other god was able to give anything. People were enslaved to them, out of fear. It is a pity that many people still live in fear of God, the Creator of the universe. Fear to be punished, fear to be rejected, fear to be confronted with their wrongdoing, fear to be chastised. A fearful life is not a life that pleases God. Where fear is present, faith leaves. They do not go together.

Now of course, what the Bible calls the 'fear of the Lord' has nothing to do with being afraid but everything with being in awe of God, with revering Him, with showing our dependence on Him, with showing Him respect. As a matter of fact,

The fear of the Lord is the beginning of wisdom, and knowledge of the Holy One is understanding (Proverbs 9:10, NIV).

We have nothing to fear but we have much to respect. Respect is a core value within Christianity. The Bible calls for mutual respect between parents and children, between spouses, and between us and God. I wrote extensively about that in my book 'Respectfully Yours'.

Throughout the Old Testament we can read that people were often afraid of God, not because they revered Him but because they disobeyed Him by running after other gods. Nowadays, we have nothing to fear because God loves us and He forgives us and He cares for us. We can enjoy His protection. That is, unless we run after other gods.

When that happens we purposely leave His protective covering and in doing so, we open the door for the enemy to enter our lives. It might hurt, but it would be good to ask ourselves whether there are indeed other gods in our lives. Things that take up a lot of our time, things that cost a lot of money, things that occupy our thoughts etc. etc. It might hurt, but it would be good to ask ourselves whether we live in divided loyalty toward God. Don't think because we live in modern times that the other gods are gone. The demonic realm is very active, maybe even more so now that Christianity has spread all over the world. The continent where Christianity was first grounded is now leaving the ways of the Lord en masse.

When Jesus came to earth in the form of a man, He represented God the Father and He did it well. He went around doing good and healing all who were oppressed by the devil. That should not shock us, people had been worshiping other gods for centuries and generational curses were a common thing. Just as much as they are today. Jesus came to see what was lost and to restore what was broken. He came to reconcile a lost and lonely generation of His own people to the Father, the God of their ancestors. And maybe the most amazing and earth-shaking thing was that He came to the earth to speak about truth.

Whenever He opened His mouth, truth came out. There was nothing false in Him. Jesus is the truth. He spoke about the Father and made a way for people to restore their broken relationship with God the Father. He came to set people free from the demonic realm, from darkness. The apostle John says it like this,

Now the message that we have heard from his Son and announce is this: God is light, and there is no darkness at all in him (1 John 1:5).

There is no darkness at all in God! So, let me put it plainly: if we experience darkness of some sort in our lives, the enemy is at work. His works are clear: depression, violence, accidents, sickness, oppression, fear, worry, anxiety, sin, wickedness, lust, and all kinds of other evil things. The other gods are from the realm of darkness and that is exactly what they bring with them if we give them a chance to operate in our lives. In God, however, there is no darkness at all. Our lives should reflect that attribute as we can read in Ephesians 5:8-9,

You yourselves used to be in the darkness, but since you have become the Lord's people, you are in the light. So you must live like people who belong to the light, for it is the light that brings a rich harvest of every kind of goodness, righteousness, and truth.

Please, read that whole chapter if you want to know for sure what 'living in the light' means, from a biblical perspective.

Meditate on the following:

- *Living in the light means…*
- *Are there any 'dark' areas in my life that I need to deal with?*

Journal your thoughts:

14

He is merciful

Our God is merciful and tender. He will cause the bright dawn of salvation to rise on us.

Luke 1:78

When I first started dating my boyfriend, who later became my husband, he proposed a trip on his BMW motorcycle to Rome. We crossed the Alps in knee deep snow, froze nearly to death (well, that was how it felt for me), and arrived safely in the beautiful city of Rome.

Rome is famous for having amazing foods such as hams, cheeses, fresh vegetables, spaghetti, lasagna, pizza and gelato. This capital of Italy is well known for historic sites such as the Colosseum, Trevi Fountain and Vatican City and we visited as many tourist sites as possible in the few days we had on that trip. The ancient Roman Empire was primarily a polytheistic civilization, which meant that people recognized and worshiped multiple gods and goddesses.

The main gods and goddesses in Roman culture were Jupiter, Juno, and Minerva. The presence and influence of gods and goddesses were integral parts of life in the Roman empire. The people of Rome built temples to their gods and observed rituals and festivals to honor and celebrate them. The Roman gods cared little about the morality of the people, quite a contrast with the God of Israel.

We are often quick to point a finger at other civilizations and cultures when it comes to worshiping other gods, but on our European continent we have quite a history of gods and goddesses influencing our culture and society, even to this day. Just think about the names of the seven days that make up a week. We do not use Hebrew names, but names that originated after the planets of Hellenistic astrology such as Sun, Moon, and Saturn. We use names that are derived from Roman, Germanic and Norse mythology such as Tiw (Tuesday), Odin (Wednesday), Thor (Thursday), and Frigga (Friday).

In the same way we have gotten accustomed to activities that are normal in our societies today but abnormal in the Kingdom of God. Think about divorce and remarrying. Think about living our lives without a proper day of rest after every six days of work. Think about dishonoring our parents, gossiping, envying what others have, allowing and even promoting abortion, and so on and so on. Many Christians will not even blink twice to participate in such practices. I am not writing this to judge anyone, but to show how far we have gone away from God's standard of living.

The Bible makes it quite clear what the consequences will be when we overstep those boundaries. Ephesians 5:3-5,

Since you are God's people, it is not right that any matters of sexual immorality or indecency or greed should even be mentioned among you. Nor is it fitting for you to use language which is obscene, profane, or vulgar. Rather you should give thanks to God. You may be sure that no one who is immoral, indecent, or greedy (for greed is a form of idolatry) will ever receive a share in the Kingdom of Christ and of God.

We might not be aware of serving other gods, but in a sense we do when we are engaged in one or more of the above mentioned activities and that goes from greed to immorality to using bad language. The whole spectrum of sin that no one wants to talk about today.

When looking at all the historical accounts, from the Israelites as well as any other people group, tribe or nation, it becomes clear that we all made mistakes, that we have all gone astray, which is no surprise. In 1 Corinthians 12:2 it is written,

You know that while you were still heathen, you were led astray in many ways to the worship of lifeless idols.

You were led astray in many ways. Well, Paul wasn't just looking back, he also had prophetic insight. People are still being led astray in many ways to worship lifeless idols. Maybe the idols are no longer the graven images with the grim faces, but they are the spirits (or demons) behind occult practices, philosophies, ideologies, addictions, cravings, greed, and lust. Anything that has set itself up against the morals and spiritual principles of God's Word. Anything or anyone that has set itself up against the God of the Bible and His Anointed One, Jesus Christ. Psalms 2:1-3 (NLT) is a prophecy about this attitude of rebellion against God.

Why are the nations so angry? Why do they waste their time with futile plans? The kings of the earth prepare for battle; the rulers plot together against the Lord and against his anointed one. "Let us break their chains," they cry, "and free ourselves from slavery to God."

This is the lie behind all worship of other gods. People believe the cunning and deceiving lie of Satan and think that they need to be freed from slavery to the God of the universe. But in reality people will end up being slaves to Satan, being slaves to all kinds of addictions, to fear, anxiety, and worry. They end up being slaves to their credit cards or to prescription drugs. I encounter people, especially Christians, who have more knowledge more about the side effects of their medications than they know about the healing power of God and His Word!

This is not what God has in mind for us. He wants us to be free from the concerns of this world that draw us away from Him if we are not careful. He wants us to come home to Him in a loving relationship. He desires to talk to us, to guide and direct us with His Holy Spirit. When Jesus left the earth, He did not leave us as orphans. He sent us the Holy Spirit, the Spirit of Truth to be with us forever. The Spirit of the living God is the seal of ownership for everyone who trusts Jesus for his or her salvation. What a concept, a concept that goes way beyond good story telling, because everyone who has received this Spirit can testify that it is a life-changing event when that happens.

Looking back at my own life, I can see that all of our travels and, in reality, also all of our searching brought us back to God, the One and only true God of the Bible. The Creator of heaven and earth, Lord of the universe. A God so far away and yet so close. A glorious God with many names and yet so personal and intimate, He calls us His children.

His supremacy is unequaled, unsurpassed, and undeniably true. All other forces are ultimately subject to Him and His judgment. The Bible says it is a terrible thing to fall into the hands of the living God. Not for followers of Jesus, for that will be a homecoming event, but for those that willfully reject Him. The same is true for the wicked and evil forces of darkness, for the demons of hell and the spirits of darkness.

The question today is real and also very personal: Whom will you love and serve with all of your heart and all of your strength? As the times we live in are becoming darker and more dangerous, please make up your mind to serve Him only. Make sure to leave no room for compromise. Close the door to any form of idolatry. Keep the other gods out, forever! Why not be part of the generation that radically follows to the Lord?

He died for all, so that those who live should no longer live for themselves, but only for him who died and was raised to life for their sake (2 Corinthians 5:15).

Meditate on the following:

- *Where am I in my journey towards the Father heart of God?*
- *Are there steps I need to take?*

Journal your thoughts:

15

The supremacy of Christ

All glory to him who alone is God, our Savior through Jesus Christ our Lord. All glory, majesty, power, and authority are his before all time, and in the present, and beyond all time! Amen.

Jude 25

Well, so much being said about the first commandment. The main message was and is that we should have no other gods before Him. That takes regular self-reflection and a deep look into our own lives to see whether there are activities, things or thoughts that take up precious time. Time we could and should spend with Him, who gave His life for us, so that we could live in fellowship with Him. The apostle John wrote,

And we know that the Son of God has come, and he has given us understanding so that we can know the true God. And now we live in fellowship with the true God because we live in fellowship with his Son, Jesus Christ. He is the only true God, and he is eternal life. Dear children, keep away from anything that might take God's place in your hearts (1 John 5:20-21, NLT).

So that we can know the true God. It is possible, for everyone on the face of the earth, to get to know the true God, who wants to be known. I want to end this book with the exhortation about the supremacy of Christ as we can read it in Colossians 1:15-20,

Christ is the visible likeness of the invisible God.

He is the first-born Son, superior to all created things.

For through him God created everything in heaven and on earth, the seen and the unseen things, including spiritual powers, lords, rulers, and authorities.

God created the whole universe through him and for him.

Christ existed before all things, and in union with him all things have their proper place.

He is the head of his body, the church; he is the source of the body's life.

He is the first-born Son, who was raised from death, in order that he alone might have the first place in all things.

For it was by God's own decision that the Son has in himself the full nature of God.

Through the Son, then, God decided to bring the whole universe back to himself. God made peace through his

*Son's blood on the cross and so brought back to himself
all things, both on earth and in heaven.*

AMEN.

Appendix

The Core Values of Christianity

But this is the covenant that I will make with the house of Israel after those days, says the Lord: I will put My law in their minds, and write it on their hearts; and I will be their God, and they shall be My people.

Jeremiah 31:33 (NKJV)

As you can read in the following section (How it all began) the ten books I have written based on the Ten Commandments represent the core values of a dedicated and fruitful Christian life. Core values are fundamental beliefs that are being lived out in our daily behavior. They can help us understand the difference between right and wrong and navigate us through the difficult challenges of life.

Now, of course this is the work of the Holy Spirit whom Jesus has freely given to everyone who has put their faith in Him. The Holy Spirit is our Teacher, Counselor, and Comforter. He gives us revelation about the Word of God. Reading the Bible and conversing with the Holy Spirit are essential ingredients of the daily life of a believer. If we fail to do so, we miss out on spiritual growth and we will be left stuck in a place.

In all ten books in this series we have looked at what the Holy Spirit wants to do in and through us. The letter kills, the Spirit gives life. Each book deals with one of the Ten Commandments and teaches us a spiritual principle that is valuable in our faith walk.

Although the Ten Commandments have not changed, the way we make them come true is totally different under the new covenant. Merely obeying or keeping a set of rules can turn into legalism. However, making the teachings come true by fulfilling them in daily life is a whole different story, as Jesus had to explain many times. The apostle John got it. He wrote:

Dear friends, I am not writing a new commandment for you; rather it is an old one you have had from the very beginning. This old commandment—to love one another—is the same message you heard before. Yet it is also new. Jesus lived the truth of this commandment, and you also are living it. For the darkness is disappearing, and the true light is already shining (1 John 2:7-8, NLT).

Do you see that? Jesus lived the truth of the commandments. I believe we are called to do the same. It is the way to push back darkness!

So, allow me to summarize the ten books in this series in what I like to call the 'Ten Core Values' of a dedicated and fruitful Christian life. No longer is the emphasis on dos and don'ts but on what a life, led by the Holy Spirit, could be like.

And remember, the Ten Core Values are summed up in one word and that is **LOVE.**

1. **LOYALTY**
    Our loyalty is to God alone and we will not be distracted by the concerns of this world.

2. **WORSHIP**
    Our gratefulness and devotion towards God express themselves in a lifestyle of worship.

3. **PRESENCE**
    We seek the presence of God on a daily basis, His presence brings peace, healing, and revelation.

4. **REST**
    We practice sabbatical rest on a daily, weekly, monthly and annual basis and experience a blessed balance in our daily lives.

5. **RESPECT**
    We show respect to our parents, children and God and at the same time are deserving of respect which will provide us with a long and healthy life.

6. **LIFE**

We advocate the protection of life, from life in the womb to life of the elderly.

7. **FAITHFULNESS**

We are being faithful to our spouses and to God.

8. **GENEROSITY**

We live a life of generosity which is the key to a blessed life.

9. **TRUTH**

We will stand up for truth and boldly proclaim the values and principles of the Bible.

10. **WISDOM**

We do not desire the things of this world, but seek after spiritual virtues such as wisdom.

How it all began

It was during the summer of 2004 that I received the personal call to write my first book 'Sacred Sabbath'. Actually, it was the first time I specifically 'heard' the Holy Spirit speaking to me. I came to faith in 2001, so I was still a relatively new believer at that time. Hearing Him speak so clearly excited me!

And so the journey began. I eagerly commenced my first humble effort to write a book and more so, to write a book in a language other than my mother tongue. Shortly after that exciting encounter I clearly heard the Holy Spirit's whisper again: 'I want you to do all ten.' And so the book series about the Ten Commandments in the 21st century began to take shape during the winter seasons that my husband and I resided in Southern California.

I enjoyed the writing process and I feared it at the same time. I struggled, cried, procrastinated, and yet dared to celebrate little victories. I doubted my writing abilities, my choice of words, and my knowledge of proper grammar, but I never doubted the words the Lord spoke to my heart that summer. I worked relentlessly on this book series.

Looking back, I can clearly see how bumpy that road has been. When my American publisher went out of business, I tried to find another publisher, or an agent for that matter, who would dare to pick up on my work. At that time my husband and I no longer divided our time between California and the Netherlands. We had permanently moved back to Europe. It turned out to be very difficult to establish contact with American publishers, so I decided to self-publish the remaining books in the series. Giving up was not an option.

At the beginning of this journey I had no idea it would take me more than nineteen years to finish the writing of ten books. There were bouts of procrastination and discouragement, but nevertheless I continued writing. I had no idea what the title of each book was going to be and that the variety of topics would turn out to be so practical and applicable in daily life. Practical and applicable yes, but even more so: prophetic in nature. Why prophetic?

Because I believe our society today is in dire need of God's living and active Word in ways that can be understood by all. The educated and uneducated, the rich and the poor, the thinkers and the doers, the sinners and the saints. His Word has not lost any of its power and purpose. On the contrary, as the 'end of this age' is nearing, we need the truth and guidance of His Word more than ever before.

While working on 'True Worshipers' back in 2020, life as the world knew it was put on hold. The Covid virus, or rather the subsequent worldwide government measures, paralyzed most activities related to writing and publishing books. No speaking engagements, no conferences, no book table at churches, nothing. It was quite difficult to maintain momentum, but I kept on writing. I had to. Simply because ever since that August morning in 2004 I had seen the social and spiritual decline in our societies. For many people biblical principles and values were no longer seen as the foundation for life in our Western world. Slowly but surely God's standard for living had been replaced by the common pagan standard of living: it is my life, I can do what I want. This is of course not how God wants us to live.

There certainly is a proper balance between law, grace, and freedom. In all of the books in this series I have emphasized the fact that, although we no longer live under law, we are to obey the law of Christ which means we must be guided by what the Holy Spirit wants to do in our lives. It is no longer about what we *cannot* or *should not* do, but about what the Holy Spirit wants to do through us. So, not stealing becomes generous giving, not giving false testimony becomes speaking truth, and not using the Lord's name in vain becomes using His name for righteous purposes. The Holy Spirit guides us in the way we should live, if we let Him.

For centuries, and maybe still so today, religious people have been going around pointing out the shortcomings in others. Although there is value in warning people that their sins will lead to death… this is *not* the Good News we are called to share. On the contrary. I sincerely believe we should go around pointing out that there is a way to receive forgiveness, grace, and a new beginning, a new life. A life that is eternally good.

I have made this call to preach the Good News very practical in all of my books that make up this series. Our lives should be the sermon that people hear, the letter that people read, and the picture that people see. We can talk all we want, but if we do not walk the talk, the talk is useless, even damaging. If good sermons had the power to change the world, the world would have been a better place long ago, because there is certainly a lot of good preaching out there.

Don't get me wrong; if you are called to preach, for crying out loud do it. Don't stop. The problem is not with the preaching in itself, but with the general idea most unbelievers have about Christians. A preconceived idea maybe, but nonetheless not a pretty picture. I am not blaming anyone, but I think we all know that in worldly circles Christians are quite often considered boring, hypocrite, old fashioned, straight, judgmental, extreme, etc. etc. Now, I am not sure how we got all these labels, but it could change.

I believe that God wants us to be *in* this world, but not *of* this world. We have to be different, we have to stand out, we have to live by godly values and principles. Just as much as He wanted the ancient Israelites to be a holy people, set apart for a different life and for different purposes, amidst pagan and often hostile neighbors. One of these purposes was of course bringing forth the Jewish Messiah, Yeshua, our Lord and Savior.

As modern-day believers, we are called to invite people into a relationship with God the Father through the Messiah and to enter the Kingdom of God, that is the realm where His will is being done. A spiritual kingdom in which we live by rules and values that differ greatly from the values in the world. The closer we are getting to the return of Christ, the clearer it becomes that the morals of both realities are opposites. Therefore, we should not mix worldly ideas with biblical values and principles. Such blending will turn into a deadly poisonous belief system that completely destroys the credibility of Christianity and thus of God.

Throughout history we can see that people often ignored the warnings, and if there ever was a time of divided loyalties, it is definitely now in the 21st century. Sad to say, but we have often tolerated sin, ungodliness, lawlessness and destruction to enter our lives, in every possible way. However, we are called to remain standing. We need courage, we need divine guidance, and we need a better understanding of the application of God's Word in our daily lives in order to remain standing in an evil world. It is my hope and prayer that this book series will provide practical and applicable biblical truths that will help us to not just survive, but to thrive in a society that is rapidly sinking deeper and deeper into troubled waters.

Do I have all the answers? No! But what I do know is that every believer needs encouragement, daily. Encouragement for daily living out our faith. Encouragement to run the race well. Encouragement to be a living testimony of God's goodness and love. And thank God, the Bible always had, and still has, the answers and cure to make for a healthy person and a healthy society. The Bible, that is the Old and the New Testament. I hope and pray that throughout this book series it has become clear that the Ten Commandments have not lost any value over time. Let me rephrase that, I believe they are more important than we can ever imagine and that is why I would like to call them the core values of the Christian faith.

A core value is a principle or belief that a person or organization views as being of central importance. I feel free to say that the Ten Commandments describe the core values of a dedicated Christian life. No, that doesn't mean we print them out and hang 'm on the wall in our homes, although that might be a great reminder of the spiritual principles that are the foundation for these commandments. The core values are rooted in love, for God is love.

It is my sincere prayer and hope that we will be able to live out these core values in a life a love, for

Love does no wrong to others, so love fulfills the requirements of God's law (Romans 13:10, NLT).

Bibliography

Also available in English:

First Love, *Embracing the challenge to pursue faithful relationships (2022)*

Love, till death do us part. Such words, promises, and vows… do they still mean anything at all in our world today? Is it possible to love and keep on loving? Is it possible to be faithful to the end?

Let's be honest, we have messed up big time when it comes to loving each other as human beings. We even messed up loving God. We have often failed to keep our promises, we have given in to temptations, and we have betrayed and hurt each other in many ways. Love has been replaced with lust, faithfulness with fantasy, and purity with perversity in our society today. This did not happen overnight, of course. It has been a slow decline of values and morals that were based on biblical principles and teachings.

When God said: 'Do not commit adultery', He was serious and He still is. Because our limited human love fails us, we need His divine love in our lives in order to be able to love others. It all starts with receiving His love, with renewing our understanding of that love, and with refreshing the way we love Him back. What God wants to establish in our spiritual lives, He will surely use in our day-to-day natural circumstances. After reading this book, you will:

- have a better understanding of God's love for people
- know that you are loved by God
- feel encouraged about refreshing your relationship with God, your spouse, and other people
- be inspired to love others as God loves you
- be able to ban boredom from your life
- be determined to remain faithful until the end.

True Worshipers, *Answering the father's call for a lifestyle of pure devotion* (2020)

2021 Illumination Book Awards Bronze Medal Winner
'Christian Living'

We never thought it could happen in just a few weeks, certainly not on a worldwide scale. But it did. Our churches had to close their doors, although temporarily, due to government regulations in response to a virus epidemic.

That brings us to a realistic and probing question. What would be left of our modern-day Christianity when all is taken away: the buildings, the meetings, the money, the power, the titles, the theology, the music, and the concerts? What would be left? We might find ourselves on our knees again, without anything. No effects, no band, no structure, no liturgy to follow. Just us, on the floor… waiting for God to speak, waiting for Him to come. After more than two thousand years of Christianity we might find ourselves bowing down again, empty-handed, with nothing but our time and lives to give Him.

Jesus prophesied that the time was coming when by the power of God's Spirit people would worship the Father as He really is, offering Him the true worship He so desires. Have you ever wondered what true worship would be like? It begins where idolatry ends. Yes, it will take a powerful move of the Holy Spirit to have our institutionalized Christianity make the transition into relational Christianity. And yes, this process starts in the heart of every believer. Will you answer the Father's call for a lifestyle of pure devotion?

In My Name, *Inviting God's holy presence in daily situations* (2018)

It is one thing to claim we don't use the Lord's name in vain, but what do we do? Are we bringing honor to His name? Do we have a genuine love for His name? And most of all, is everything we do and say then, done in His name? The letter of the Old Testament law says 'do not use the Lord's name in vain', Jesus however urges every believer to 'honor His holy name'. We will find out how such a commandment can become practical and applicable for believers today, not by focusing on what we cannot and should not do, but by focusing on what the Holy Spirit wants to do in us and through us. May we use God's name with power, purpose and reverence in effective ministry all over the world and in doing so be a generation that fulfills the ancient scriptures right here and now in the 21st century.

Spirit of Truth, *Finding certainty and standing firm in a troubled world* (2016)

One of the most famous questions ever asked in the history of mankind, was the one Pilate desperately confronted Jesus with: 'and what is truth?' In Spirit of Truth the reader is being challenged to answer Pilate's question and to go on a quest for that one certainty that would settle all dispute, all error, all doubt: Truth, with a capital T. Find out the importance of living and speaking truthfully and discover how to stand up for biblical values and principles in a troubled world that seems to have taken a free fall into lawlessness.

My Neighbor's House, *Digging Deeper to Find the Treasure That will Satisfy the Longing of Your Heart* (2013)

What do we do with the old pages of Exodus 20 in this current age and time? How do we apply them in our daily life? It is one thing to say, 'Oh, I don't envy my neighbor, his house, car, or wife. I don't desire what someone else has.' But come to think of it, what do you desire? What are the desires of your heart? Are you passionate for the right things? In this fifth book in the Ten Commandments series, you'll learn how to desire meaningful things and apply God's word to everyday life.

Grace of Giving, *Turning the Key to Enter & Experience Fullness of Life* (2011)

2011 Reader's Favorite Gold Medal Award Winner
'Best Christian Non-Fiction'

It is one thing to claim we do not steal, but the logical next question would be, 'What do we do? How do we go from merely obeying such a command to fulfilling it in our daily lives? Is it truly possible to become a cheerful giver?' In her award-winning book Grace of Giving, the fourth one in this series, Marja answers these questions by taking an in-depth look at the commandment 'do not steal.' The author offers a liberating and fresh insight on the eighth commandment as she shares how we can leave behind the way of the thief, which always cries for more, more, more. In her known step-by-step method, she slowly reveals the way of the Master, which is cheerful, abundant, and costly giving that will lead us into a life in all its fullness!

Breath of Life, *A Journey into Origin and Purpose of Spirit, Soul, and Body* (2008)

As human beings, we are made in the image and likeness of God. We are uniquely designed triune beings: spirit, soul, and body, yet one. The author takes the reader on a journey to our earthly beginnings and beyond. Based on biblical concepts and a surprising array of scriptures, she has painted an artistic picture of a colorful and loving God who is the source of all life. Breath of life is based on the commandment not to commit murder and it deals with the very core of our existence: life before and after conception.

Respectfully Yours, *Revealing God's Truth about Well-being and a Long Life* (2007)

Respectfully Yours is the second book in a series about the Ten Commandments in the twenty-first century. Based on the commandment to honor our parents, it deals with a much broader aspect of family life—the mutual respect between God, parents, and children. The letter of the Old Testament bursts into life as author Marja explains the new way of the Spirit. This book is not just a short and easy-to-understand study; it is a thought-provoking page turner that will transform your view of the parent-child relationship!

Sacred Sabbath, *God's Way to Multiply Our Time and Restore Our Joy* (2006)

Sacred Sabbath is the first book in a series about the Ten Commandments in the twenty-first century. It is a short and easy to understand study that doles out profound nuggets of wisdom to anyone who wants to live the life God had in mind when He created mankind. It explains how we can fulfill The Law in a spirit of love just as Jesus did. Sacred Sabbath will lead the reader into an inward change rather than toward an outward experience.

Visit the author at www.marjameijers.com